LAW SCHOOL

A Guide for the Perplexed

D. C. Zook

SHANTIWALA BOOKS
Berkeley, CA

Text copyright © 2017 by D. C. Zook
All rights reserved.
Published by Shantiwala Books (Berkeley, CA)
Cover design by James at GoOnWrite.com
ISBN: 1947609076
ISBN-13 (print): 9781947609075
ISBN-13 (E-book): 9781947609051

To the one and only Willie Claiborne Brown, Ph.D.,
Professor Emeritus, Division of Biological Sciences,
University of California, San Diego, whose words of
wisdom might not be law, but they should be.

TABLE OF CONTENTS

Preface   Pondering Perplexity   vii

Chapter 1   So you think you want to go to law school?   1
Chapter 2   What's the difference between law school
            and graduate school?   5
Chapter 3   Why study law?   10
Chapter 4   Should I go straight to law school from
            undergrad?   17
Chapter 5   What do you mean there's no
            such thing as pre-law?   21
Chapter 6   Can I go to law school to change
            my current career?   25
Chapter 7   Should I work as a paralegal to
            improve my chances of getting in?   28
Chapter 8   I've made my decision: Where do I start?   31
Chapter 9   How important is my GPA?   34
Chapter 10 Whom should I ask for letters of
            recommendation?   39
Chapter 11 How should I approach the LSAT?   44
Chapter 12 How should I write my
            personal statement?   48
Chapter 13 Which schools should I apply to?   52
Chapter 14 Which school should I choose?   56

Chapter 15   Is it really worth the money to go?   61
Chapter 16   Is there any way to avoid all that debt?   65
Chapter 17   What's the point of law school?   69
Chapter 18   Should I consider a joint degree?   72
Chapter 19   What kinds of law will I study?   76
Chapter 20   What about human rights law?   81
Chapter 21   What about international law?   86
Chapter 22   What about comparative law?   92
Chapter 23   What's law school like?
               The first year (1L)   98
Chapter 24   What's law school like?
               The second year (2L)   105
Chapter 25   What's law school like?
               The third year (3L)   110
Chapter 26   What's the bar exam all about?   112
Chapter 27   Do I have to take the bar exam?   116
Chapter 28   What's a day in the life of a lawyer?   120
Chapter 29   What if I don't want to be a lawyer?   124
Chapter 30   What's clerking all about?   129
Chapter 31   Do I have to choose between
               fighting for justice and making money?   133
Chapter 32   Those lawyer jokes—Are lawyers
               really bad people?   138
Chapter 33   What does the (legal) future hold?   142
Chapter 34   Can you tell me an inspiring story
               about law?   146
Chapter 35   Can you recommend things about law
               for me to read, see, and hear?   150

Epilog   From perplexity to clarity   173
About the Author   175

PREFACE

PONDERING PERPLEXITY

Many an astute reader may have noticed that the title of this guidebook is inspired, respectfully and humorously, by the work of the great philosopher Maimonides (c. 1135-1204). Maimonides wrote his great philosophical tract, which in English carries the title *The Guide for the Perplexed*, around 1190, and wrote it as something of a letter to one of his students, as a way of trying to resolve and explain the seemingly impenetrable complexities embedded in many passages of religious scripture. By providing a key with which to understand the complexities and mysteries of scriptural passages, Maimonides wanted to transform perplexity into clarity. Maimonides also wrote a separate corpus of opinions on Jewish law, so I figured given his link to law, and given his intent to help a student work through the perplexities of the divinely-inspired theological universe, it seemed a good model to do roughly the same for a guidebook to help negotiate the bewildering complexities of law school, for those who perhaps seek to enter its hallowed halls. I've spent many an hour with many a student going over the things you will find in this book, and at some point I simply thought there must be lots of students (and non-students) out there who have the same questions. And so, I sat down one day and starting writing this book, which I now offer to you, dear reader, in the hope that what might first appear to be perplexing and daunting gently becomes something tangible and comforting. The decision to go to law school is a decision that can potentially set the course for the rest of your life, so there is something both exhilarating and frightening in making this choice. This book is intended to help you make that choice, in a way that hopefully gets rid of the frightening parts and leaves only the exhilarating ones. Law school isn't for everybody, but it is certainly for somebody. Is that somebody you? Read on, my friend, for the answer to that question can be found in the pages that follow.

CHAPTER 1

SO YOU THINK YOU WANT TO GO TO LAW SCHOOL?

A h, yes—Law School. The name itself conjures up so many different images and ideas. One thing that can be said for certain about law school, however, is that whether you are an undergraduate student contemplating what comes next after you graduate or someone who has already walked a ways down the road of a career that no longer inspires you, the decision to go law school is not one to be taken lightly. I've come across far too many people who *think* they want to go to law school, but in reality they have no idea what law school is or why they want to go. For many, it's the default choice: they don't want to go into business, they don't want to be a doctor, and so...law school it is! But here's the thing: this is a terrible way to make what could be a career-defining, life-altering decision. If you want to go to law school to become a lawyer, then you should at least know what a lawyer is and what a lawyer does, or what law school is all about, before you even think to make the decision to apply to law school. And by the way—no, you don't have to be a lawyer if you go to law school. There are other options, but we'll get to those a bit later. For now, the main point I want to make right from the start is this: if you do decide to go to law school, then you should at least be as well-informed as possible when it comes time to make the choice. And that, my legally perplexed friends, is what this exquisitely epic and audaciously awesome guide is all about.

The first thing I should probably do to best prepare you for law school is to destroy your dreams. Not all of them, mind you—don't worry, your unicorns are safe. For now. But whatever dreams you may have about being a law student or a lawyer that are based on images you've seen in the media, whether on the big screen or the small, you'll need to jettison those right away. I know this will hurt a bit when I tell you this, but nearly all of the things you see on whatever size screen you watch when you want to be entertained have very little connection to reality. This is especially true for the programs that call themselves reality shows. It is also especially true for pretty much any show or movie ever made that has something to do with being a lawyer.

In a day in the life of a lawyer, for instance, you will never solve an unbelievably complicated case in sixty minutes, and you will rarely if ever obtain justice in such a way that concludes with an inspiring battle of heated courtroom drama in which you trounce your courtroom adversary so definitively that members of the jury weep, the judge swoons, and pigs fly, at least until the cows come home (because as any Midwesterner will tell you, cows won't tolerate that kind of outlandish behavior from pigs). You will also never find a Hollywood movie or Netflix series with a title like "Brief Writer," in which our hero spends gruelingly long days writing one legal brief after another, making sure for an exciting conclusion that she checks every source reference to ensure that each is formatted according to the rules of proper legal citation. Nor will your day as a lawyer consist of high-powered and stimulating conversations full of witty one-liners from all the quirky, well-dressed, and attractive people that amazingly ended up in the same law firm. To make the law entertaining, it has to be heavily edited. Please do not make the life-altering decision to go to law school based on images that for the most part bear little resemblance to the reality of what it is like to be a lawyer.

Being a lawyer may not be consistently entertaining, but that doesn't mean it won't be consistently compelling. Not every day, of course—you'll still have plenty of days when you glance down at your legal pad and realize you've written *kill me now* or *make it stop* where there should normally be professional notes and insightful commentary. But being a lawyer or working in a law-related field can be an extraordinarily interesting career—provided you are genuinely interested in how the law actually works. In other words, having destroyed your dreams first, the good news is that you can easily restock your dream drawer with new dreams, albeit this time, ones that might actually come true. Don't get me wrong—you still might end up working with people you find insufferably dull or obnoxious, or you might end up in an unbearably stressful and competitive work environment, or you might find yourself in soul-crushingly long and soporific meetings where you actually imagine taking a jackhammer to your own skull just to escape the tedium in which you are mired. But the good news is that all of those things can happen in any job and any career—law isn't unique in its capacity to turn a good day bad with surprising swiftness and ease—so don't let any of that deter you from becoming a lawyer. The only thing you need to focus on for now is making sure that your decision to go to law school is the right decision to make.

I emphasize that for many reasons. Once you make the decision to go to law school, you will find very quickly that money is involved. A lot of money. I will go into detail about all of this in the pages to come, but for now, consider just the initial costs of applying to law school and paying for LSAT prep classes and paying to take the LSAT, among other things. All of that adds up very quickly. There is probably no worse feeling to experience than to go through all the effort and expenditure to get into law school, only to find out about three weeks into your first semester that you've made a terrible mistake. And no, at that point you can't ask for a refund. All you have accomplished at that point is that you have wasted a lot of time and money on something you *thought* you wanted to do, without ever giving your decision the serious reflection you should have in the first place. Law school may indeed be the right choice for you, but you'll be so much further ahead of the game and so much happier right from the start if you show up as a 1L (first-year law student) and know for sure you're in the right place at the right time. If this guidebook helps make that happen for you, then it has all been worth the effort for me.

CHAPTER 2

WHAT'S THE DIFFERENCE BETWEEN LAW SCHOOL AND GRADUATE SCHOOL?

While this isn't technically a trick question, it is possible to consider law school a form of graduate school, if you are using the term "graduate school" to mean any educational program you pursue after you finish your undergraduate degree. But in a more specific sense, postgraduate programs are for the most part divided into two separate but not necessarily mutually exclusive camps: professional programs and research programs. For most people, it certainly isn't intuitively obvious what the main difference is between these two types of programs, as it seems to imply that you won't do research in a professional program and you won't do anything professional in a research program. Neither of those is true, so perhaps a bit of explanation is in order.

Professional programs are programs that are designed to teach you a specific set of skills that are standard for a specific profession, and also to facilitate your entry into the particular profession you have chosen. Law school is certainly a professional school, since it teaches you the standard skills and knowledge base that any lawyer would need to know and also uses its vast networks to help you find your way to the legal occupation of your legal desire. But law school isn't the only example of a professional school. Public policy schools are professional programs, as are business schools, public health and medical schools, architecture and city planning schools, and even many social welfare programs. All of these programs have a specific degree attached to them, and the degree you earn entitles you to identify your profession by the credentials afforded by that degree. Law school gives you a J.D. (Juris Doctor, a Doctor of Law, but confusing insofar as a J.D. is not considered a doctoral degree). Public policy gives you an MPP (Master of Public Policy), public health gives you an MPH (Master of Public Health), medical school gives you an MD (Medical Doctor), social welfare gives you an MSW (Master of Social Work), and so on (too bad there isn't an MASW, or Master of Anti-Social Work, which would entitle you, indeed require you, to be professionally rude at all times). Most professional programs require you to pay a professional fee each year on top of your standard tuition. This is money you pay for the professional training in your program, which is often seen as a separate element beyond the educational curriculum of the program you are in.

Graduate school, on the other hand, consists primarily of research-based programs and degrees. Depending on the field you choose, you can end up with an MA (Master of Arts) or MS (Master of Science) or even MFA (Master of Fine Arts, amusing only insofar as it implies that someone with an MA lacks a certain amount of finesse), or should you choose to go for the long-haul, a PhD (Doctor of Philosophy). You can very quickly see one crucial difference between graduate school and professional school. If you earn a PhD, you also need to state what your PhD is in—history, political science, sociology, etc. If you go to law school, no one will ever ask you "what did you do your JD in?" Or perhaps I should say if anyone ever does ask you that, they're probably not the wisest whale in the pod, so you might want to move on to a new conversation or social circle at whatever party or social venue you are gracing at that moment. And for that tip, you're whalecom.

The distinction between these types of programs is relatively important. Research-based programs are designed to provide you with a solid foundation of all the theories, schools of thought, and research methods in your chosen field, and the main focus is on learning how to do engaged and original research in your field. Your master's thesis or doctoral dissertation is the major project through which you show not only that you can conduct original and rigorously-designed research on your own, but also, through the topic of your thesis or dissertation, that you have an area of specialization that is clearly defined. No one will ever ask you what your area of specialization was in law school, but it is an essential question when it comes to graduate school.

Professional schools have an emphasis on professional experience and building a professional resume, so things like internships and other opportunities during your studies aren't just encouraged but required. There is often but not always an emphasis on pragmatic applications and approaches, the so-called real world experience, and again, all of this is designed to help you launch a career in your chosen profession right out of the graduated gate. Professional schools are ranked partly on their ability to place their graduates into career-track positions, so they have as much an interest as you do in trying to make that happen. I'll talk more about how that happens in law school in a later chapter. For now, I'm just giving a drone's-eye descriptive overview of the educational landscape.

In case you are thinking graduate school must therefore by mired in a lack of real-world relevance and pragmatism (so called ivory-tower academia), I should point out that this would be an uncharitable assessment. Research-based degree programs are as necessary a part of the puzzle as are professional ones, and where they differ is simply in the methods and approaches they use to obtain and create information. A lawyer needs to learn a good strategy to win her or his case. A research-based scholar may instead develop a broader and more theoretical approach, for example about why some countries comply with human rights treaties more than others, or why juries are swayed by this tactics but not that, or why the rule of law is stronger in some parts of the world than in others. We need both of these perspectives to understand the complexity and the power of law.

You will certainly learn how to do legal research in law school, but law school in and of itself is not a research-driven curriculum. And in case you might be thinking you are interested in the law but don't really want to go to law school, there are actually quite a few other options for you. I'll discuss law school-related alternatives later, but for now, you might explore how different fields like political science or psychology or sociology or philosophy approach the study of law. While your friends are all binging on Netflix, you could instead pick up the hefty tome by John Rawls entitled *A Theory of Justice* and then follow that literary thread over to someone like Amartya Sen who developed an approach to episodes of economic injustice (hunger, poverty, etc.) derived in large part from Rawlsian theories, which ultimately earned him a Nobel Prize in Economics in 1998. And I would be remiss in my duties if I didn't alert you to the existence of the JSP (Jurisprudence and Social Policy) program at UC Berkeley. This is a PhD program within the law school itself, so in many ways it is the best of both worlds. It's also a most excellent program, so do have a look (and there are a few other programs like it) before you make your ultimate decision about where to go and what to do when you get there.

CHAPTER 3

WHY STUDY LAW?

U ntil you know where to look for it, it's easy not to notice just how much of the world is connected to the law. Sure, there's the speed limit sign on the highway—that's easy to spot. And if you want to have some idea of the power of law, think of your emotional reaction on that same highway when you're driving along well over the speed limit and suddenly you spot a police car. But what about your trip to the grocery store—did you get a receipt? That's technically a legal document. Did you pay in cash at the store? Next time you do, look at your currency. Somewhere on the bills you'll find the magic words "legal tender." Want to do something really cool and write an epic and awesome guide to law school and then publish it? If you do, at some point you'll have to sign a contract, which is by definition a legally binding document. Will your book hold a copyright? If so, a copyright is also part of the legal family.

Aside from those somewhat ordinary things, law shows up in nearly all of the important questions about the world around us. Is there a genocide happening in South Sudan? To answer that question, we turn to Article II of the Genocide Convention (1948), which contains the legal definition of genocide (a convention, by the way, is a multilateral treaty that is open for signature and ratification—both of which are legal acts—to any member state of the United Nations. And while I'm at it, joining the United Nations is also a legal process). Are there war crimes happening in Syria? For that, we turn to the Geneva Conventions (1949), which enumerate and define war crimes. Who has the legal authority to bring charges of war crimes and which court has jurisdiction? Only the law can provide answers to both of those questions.

In other words, so many of the questions you may have about why and how the world is the way it is, and almost all of the questions you have about justice and injustice, from the individual to the international levels, rely heavily upon the law for answers. There's actually a historical reason for that, and it relates to another type of legal document, namely a peace treaty. The Treaty of Westphalia (1648), the peace treaty that brought an end to the horribly violent and destructive Thirty Years War (1618-1648) in Europe, may not be something you've heard much about, but it is perhaps the document most responsible for the legalification of the world. What it did was create a legal basis for the concept of state sovereignty, which gave states exclusive control over their internal governance (domestic law), a governance that was in turn legally protected from outside intervention by other legally sovereign entities (international law). How important was the latter point? Well, if you pull out a copy of the UN Charter (there's an app for that) and start reading, you'll quickly come across Article 2(7), which is the non-intervention clause. In other words, the principle of non-intervention that derived from the peace of Westphalia is still a legal cornerstone of international relations. Oh, and in case you didn't catch it, the UN Charter is...wait for it...a legal document.

Don't get my wrong—Europe didn't invent law for the rest of the world. Law codes have been foundational institutions for cultures, societies, and even religions throughout human history. Jewish concepts of law, for instance, pervade the Old Testament, and don't forget the centrality in the New Testament of the trial of Jesus. The development of *shari'ah* law is a fundamental element of the Islamic community (*ummah*), while the concept of *dharma* similarly connects divine law to communities of faith in both Hinduism and Buddhism. For many historians and legal scholars, the earliest law code in human history, at least the earliest one we know of, is the Code of Hammurabi (1754 BCE). There have many other law codes throughout human history originating independently all around the world. The legal impulse, it seems, is also a human impulse. Where you find people, you will find law.

Aside from that rather wide-ranging overview, here are four specific reasons why studying law is a good and noble thing to do.

There is no justice without law. If you're one of those people who wants to fight for justice and make the world a better place—and if you are, let me say thank you—you'll quickly find that you won't get very far without a thorough grounding in the workings of the law. All acts of injustice small or large must by definition turn to the law to render justice in the face of injustice. Whether your goal is to put an end to the nauseating global market known as human sex trafficking, or to help the elderly battle ageism and exploitation, either way you are going to need to know the law and know it well. Law may not be the only thing involved in obtaining justice, but I can guarantee that without it, justice will always be incomplete, if not entirely absent.

Lawyers are essential to the proper functioning of society. I'll have more to say about lawyers later in these pages, but for now, just understand that if so many parts of everyday life relate in some way to law, then it stands to reason that lawyers play an essential role in making sure that all goes legally to plan, properly and procedurally. That's right—we *need* lawyers. More importantly, we need *good* lawyers. When Joey Ramone alerted the world that "the KKK took my baby away," he was quite right later in the song to reach out to the legal experts at the FBI because potentially the incident involved kidnapping across state lines. But even for the crimes and misdemeanors that are a little less melodic than the punkish lamentations of The Ramones, you would still be surprised at how frequently the skills of a lawyer are necessary for even the most mundane things. For pretty much any state or society in the world, it remains a truism: The better the lawyers, the better the society. So if you do end up becoming a lawyer, please remember the wise counsel of E.T.—be good.

Law is empowering. The more you learn about the law the more you will discover just how frequently people misunderstand and misuse it. I mention that because nothing disempowers a particular cause or movement more than making claims that turn out not to be valid, legally speaking. The corollary to that, of course, is that a solid knowledge of the law, and speaking with the proper knowledge of the law behind you, can be very empowering. I'll give you an example of this, one that might be a little surprising. Ever see a protest where someone is holding a sign that says, "Immigrant rights are human rights"? Well, guess what? They're wrong. It's not that immigrants forfeit their human rights and can therefore be abused and exploited by anyone with the sick inclination to do so. It's that in the world of human rights, there is no human right to immigrate to another country. Any and every country in the world has the right to refuse a person entry (yet another thing that emerged from the Treaty of Westphalia). If you are referring to the right of due process that every immigrant has in the United States, whether they crossed the border legally or not, then you should know that the right to due process is not a human right, generated by international human rights treaties, but rather a civil right generated by the US Constitution (the 14th Amendment to be specific). These may seem like oddly-specific details, but the law thrives on specificity, and having a deep and detailed knowledge of the law can make a huge difference in how seriously your message or your cause is perceived by others.

Law is hella interesting. Did you know that California has a law on the books that says it is illegal to shoot an animal from any moving vehicle unless that animal is a whale? If you're pondering how you might be able to shoot a whale from your skateboard, well, first let me say how unsettling it is that you would ponder that in the first place, and then let me clarify that the weird wording of the law came about because when the law was written in the nineteenth century, whaling was still a thing in California, and ships were considered moving vehicles. Speaking of whales and why the law is crazy interesting, I'll share with you my favorite name of any court case ever: *The Cetacean Community v. George W. Bush* (2004). Cetaceans are whales, in case you didn't know that, and this particular case involved a law suit to force the US Navy (George W. Bush would have been the commander-in-chief) to stop testing a new and very powerful sonar system that had the unfortunate effect of bursting the inner membranes of the whales, causing pain so intense that they beached themselves (which is basically whale suicide). The Ninth Circuit Court of Appeals ended up declining the case, not because, as you might suspect, the whales lacked sufficient currency to pay for their Baleen Bonds, but rather because the whales lacked proper legal standing for the case to proceed. (Standing in this case refers not to the inability of the whales to stand up, but rather to their lack of proper status as legal persons, which you need to take part in legal proceedings.) Interestingly, the Ninth Circuit Court left open the option to rehear the case if Congress were to pass legislation giving legal personhood to whales.

It isn't just the fate of whales that makes law so interesting. Did you know that you can be an outer space insurance lawyer? It's true, you can—and what an awesome business card you would have. Everything from presidential impeachment to penguins in Antarctica has a central connection to at least one legal framework. The main point here, however, is to emphasize that there are many compelling reasons to study law. But as I have also stated, just because you are interested in studying law doesn't mean that law school is necessarily the next logical step. Once you realize you are interested in pursuing the study of law, *then* you need to start thinking about whether law school is the right choice for you.

CHAPTER 4

SHOULD I GO STRAIGHT TO LAW SCHOOL FROM UNDERGRAD?

To get straight to the point: no, you shouldn't. And here's a little inside secret for you: it isn't just me who recommends you take some time off—most law schools want you to do so, too. I'm well-aware than many a person who reads this will find the whole idea of taking time off a little uncomfortable or even counter-intuitive, and for those readers who might currently be undergrads, no doubt bringing up the idea of a "gap year" might not go down well with the parental authorities, who are anxious to see you start your career as quickly as possible. To them, taking a year or two off sounds an awful lot like floundering or falling behind, and it might even sound and feel that way to you, too. And yes, I know that there have been many undergrads who have gone straight to law school and yes, they did just fine. But you know what? They're not you—only you are you. You need to figure out what is best for you, based on who you are and what you want out of life. For that, what other people did or didn't do is astonishingly irrelevant.

What I will now do is explain the reasons why taking some time off is actually a good idea, and then will finish up with a bit of advice for those who decide that in the end, they don't want to wait and want to go to law school straight from undergrad. Here we go.

The first and most important reason to take some time off is that law school is a *very* intense experience. There's a reason you don't see law students sleeping on the grass on campus. Actually there's a reason you don't see law students sleeping at all. Law school goes from 0 to 60 mph (0 to 100 kph for the metrically minded) very quickly and stays at that speed for pretty much the whole three years. So if you've ever had an inkling to travel the world or at least part of it, or make some progress on that list of must-read books or must-see movies you've been compiling, or learn how to tango (both Argentinian and Finnish styles, of course), or explore Mongolian hip-hop, or spend some quality time with or without family and friends, or quite frankly, just binge extravagantly on Netflix without feeling even a hint of guilt—then do all that before you go to law school. I can't tell you how many emails I have received from former students who went straight through to law school from undergrad, got their first legal job, and then wrote to say the one thing they miss more than anything else is the chance to just sit and read a book or watch a movie without having to think about all the messages piling up in their professional inbox and all the things they know they have to do before the workday starts again, which it does with relentless annoyance.

I realize that not everyone has the means to travel or to take time off just to indulge in fun-filled activities, but there is still every reason to take a year or two off even if your plan is to work, either to pay off student loans from undergrad days (if you have them) or to save up a bit of money as a monetary cushion before you go to law school. Even if you end up in a haplessly mundane job during your time off—one for instance that leaves you emotionally despondent for the rest of your life every time you hear the question "room for cream?"—or even in a job you actually hate, this can work to your advantage, too. Think of how happy you'll be on that first day of law school, freed from that dead-end nine-to-five job you suffered through for a whole year and will never again have to go back to. In that situation, law school for you will feel like you've won the lottery in a way that leaves you all sorts of room for cream.

One of the reasons that many a law school will encourage students to take at least a year off before coming to law school, regardless of what they do during that year, is that it gives potential law students a little something called *life experience*. Life experience is actually very useful for the study of law, because with even a little life experience, once you start reading case after case about the horrible and stupid things that people do, you will be neither surprised nor shocked and you can instead focus more intently on the matters of law that apply, which is what law school wants you to focus on. Life experience is also great for how it deepens and broadens one's perspective on pretty much everything, which makes a person that much more attractive as a candidate for law school. On a more pragmatic note, there's also the fact that if you've taken a year or two off and are still committed to law school, it means you've really thought this through and know that law school is definitely the right choice for you. Law schools like it when that happens.

Also don't overlook the fact that you can use the year off to put together your application for law school without the ongoing stress of your senior year. I'll talk later about what is involved in the application process for law school, but there is something to be said for taking some time off to concentrate fully on crafting the perfect law school application.

At the end of the day, however, if you are still one of those people who insists that you want to get started as quickly as possible and so decide to enter law school straight from your undergrad years, then all I can recommend is that you not load up the summer before you start with all sorts of prep work for law school. The most important thing for any incoming student at any law school is to arrive on the first day well-rested, fresh-faced, and ready to embrace the challenges of law school, of which there are many. If you show up tired and not fully ready to go, then early burn out becomes a real possibility. Once law school starts, taking time off really isn't a viable or professional option, so you don't want to be sitting in a law lecture half-way through your first semester, tired and uninspired, and realize only then that you really should have taken some time off.

CHAPTER 5

WHAT DO YOU MEAN THERE'S NO SUCH THING AS PRE-LAW?

While I know there are schools that offer what they call "pre-law" programs and majors, the truth of the matter is, pre-law is the unicorn of majors—it doesn't really exist, though that never stopped anyone from believing in it anyway. Unlike a pre-med program, which does exist and exists for a very specific reason, there really is no major in existence that gives you a head start or an advantageous skill-set for law school. Pre-med programs exist because you need a certain amount of medical and scientific knowledge before you can go to or even apply to medical school. Law school doesn't work that way. Law schools want you to be able to write well, think nimbly, communicate mellifluously, and dance ecstatically—okay maybe I made up the last one—but you can develop those skills in pretty much any major you choose. In fact, you can apply to law school even if you were pre-med (though conversely you can't apply to medical school if you were pre-law). There are of course other qualities that law schools want to see in a candidate, and I'll talk about those a bit later when I talk about the process of putting together your application. For now, I will just focus on what to do in your undergraduate studies to best prepare you for law school.

So what's the best major to choose to prepare you for law school? The answer is simple: whichever major is most interesting to you. There's absolutely no need to force yourself into a series of courses in a certain major just because you think it is some sort of pre-law program or because you think it is the kind of major that will look attractive to law schools. So if you've always been wanting to major in Sanskrit literature, or comparative religion, or peace and conflict studies, or theater studies, or medieval history, or cross-cultural psychology, or African music—you get the idea—please feel free to do so. Chances are that if you choose a major that you really want and that really captures your interest, you'll do very well in it, and along the way you will most certainly acquire the basic skill set that law schools are looking for in a potential candidate.

In response to the question of whether you should major in political science or legal studies, the answer is simple: do so *only* if that is what you are interested in. Don't choose them because you think it's what law schools are looking for. Law schools are going to teach you everything you need to know, so having a background in legal studies isn't really an advantage, and the number of applicants to law school that majored in political science is predictably, almost stereotypically overabundant. Why is that important? Well, consider your personal statement, which I will talk about in more detail in a later chapter. If your personal statement says something like,

"I feel my political science background and my senior thesis on the criminal justice system in America make me a strong candidate for law school," well, it's you among ten thousand other applicants who made the same choices and wrote the same thesis for the very same reasons. If your personal statement instead says something like, "The first time I read the *Ramayana* in the original Sanskrit, I felt like my soul was on fire," I think it's safe to say it's just you. Follow your passion, and don't get caught up on some formulaic path that you think will lead you to the law school of your choice.

Also, don't choose a major or clusters of classes that have a reputation for being easy at your school, just so you can keep your GPA high. Law school admissions committees are composed of smart, experienced people who have pretty much seen it all, and the easy class route to law school is one of the things they have definitely seen far too many times. So if they see that on your transcript, one thing they won't want to see is you at their law school.

Once you have chosen your major, the next thing to do is to focus on developing the sort of skill set that will be useful for you in law school. Law is a text-based field, so you will want to develop a capacity to read critically and write effectively. Reading critically means to push beyond just reading through texts to get the gist of things. It means to read and then re-read and engage with the text to find what you think are weak points or strong points, or points that you can link with other things you have already read. You should learn how to question things and how to think outside the box. Writing effectively means not only developing a clear and fluid writing style, but also, and most important of all, it means being able to write a concise and powerful thesis statement. Another word for thesis statement is *argument*, and being able to make a forceful, persuasive, and compelling argument is an absolutely essential skill in the practice of law. How important is this skill? When a student approaches me for a letter of recommendation for law school, the first thing I think of are the papers she or he wrote for my classes and how well-crafted the thesis statements were. If the thesis statements were weak and vague, and if the student didn't show real commitment to improving their ability to craft articulate and effective arguments, then I cannot in good conscience recommend them for law school. Yep, that's how important it is.

One last thing. If you decided to pursue your passion and your passion led you to a science-related field such as mathematics or integrative biology or astrophysics, then first let me say I think it's audaciously awesome that you made the choice to follow your passion. But *then* let me say that science fields are sometimes weak on letting you develop your writing skills, so when it comes time to take some electives outside your major, choose courses that will offer the opportunity for you to do so. I'm not saying that science types can't write well. Everyone knows Einstein for his science writings, for example, but his more philosophical writings are equally and eloquently inspiring. But writing a lab report or even writing a research paper along the guidelines of scientific formatting may not help you develop your skill set in a way that will be most effective for law school.

In short, what's the best major to prepare you for law school? The one that grabs your inner muse and makes you dance ecstatically—and by dance I mean craft effective arguments.

CHAPTER 6

CAN I GO TO LAW SCHOOL TO CHANGE MY CURRENT CAREER?

I t's never a good thing when you're sitting at your desk at the rent-a-clown agency, or serving another round of drinks to a couple of barftastic barflies, or singing Green Day cover songs in Spanish at a poorly attended quinceañera, and then suddenly you have that moment of realization when you say to yourself: *I can't do this anymore.* Or perhaps you got a great job in a management consulting firm but it's slowly dawning on you that management consulting just isn't your thing. It's even possible that you got a groovy job in a non-profit that does amazing work helping high school students from at-risk families stay in school, but you become increasingly aware that your salary just isn't enough to live on, especially if you are working in a place like San Francisco, where $4,000 a month in rent will get you a small space on the sidewalk from which you have a partial view of someone else's $8,000 a month studio.

Whatever the situation is that brings you to the realization that it's time for a change of plans, if you are thinking of putting law school on your list of possible options, you might have that lingering question that you don't want to ask because you're afraid to hear the answer. So I'll ask it for you: *is it too late for me to go to law school?* The answer to the question....drum roll please...is no, it's not too late for you to go to law school. In fact, there are some things that might work to your advantage if you are considering law school. One of the things that law schools try to do when putting together a cohort of entering students is choose a judicious and interesting mix of different kinds of people. Law schools actually like having older students in the entering cohort, even if you might not like the idea of being labeled an "older student." Law schools like to have older students because they bring with them a suitcase full of worldly experience that can potentially add a lot to classroom discussions. I know people that have gone to law school mid-career, which would put them, say, in their 40s, and were quite happy they did so.

If you are one of those people considering a career change that involves law school, however, the same things I said in the earlier chapters still hold true—make sure law school is the right choice to make. If it is, and you are sure of it, then by all means make that choice and never look back.

The only place where you might face a little more difficulty, if you are a person who has been out of school for a few or more than a few years, is in the application process. You'll need things like letters of recommendation (which I'll talk about soon), and while those don't necessarily have to come from professors you may have had five or ten years ago—and who might not remember who you are—you will still need letters from people who can speak to your ability to handle the rigors and challenges of law school and also to write cogently, think brilliantly, and so on.

Getting back to the academic mode can be tough if you've been out of it for a while, but let the fact that it could be a life-changing and certainly career-changing decision, and a very positive one at that, inspire you to dig deep and find the energy and commitment you need to follow through. I know a lot of people who have done it, and never a one of them has ever expressed a single regret.

CHAPTER 7

SHOULD I WORK AS A PARALEGAL TO IMPROVE MY CHANCES OF GETTING IN?

This is a question I get a lot from students interested in law school, and I certainly understand the logic behind it. If you apply to a public policy program, for instance, most of them don't just encourage you to have some professional experience before you apply, they actually require it. So it would make sense to think that, in trying to make your application stand out from the crowd in the hyper-competitive law school application process, perhaps having some experience working in a law firm will be just the thing you need to improve your chances. But before you send out a flood of resumes to law firms, hoping one of them will be seduced by what I am quite sure are your very impressive credentials, you might want to consider this inside tip: *working as a paralegal, or working in any other capacity in a law firm, will do pretty much nothing to improve your chances of getting into law school.*

Having said that, however, let me explain why you might still consider working as a paralegal, or as any other type of employee in a law firm, before you head off to law school. Working in a law firm, even if you're just filing papers or helping with paperwork or making vegan donut runs for that weird environmental lawyer everyone refers to as Hemp, can give you invaluable insight in trying to figure out if law school is really the right choice for you. For some potential law school applicants, working in a law firm seals the deal and confirms their initial inclination—*yes, I know I want to go to law school.* But for other students considering law school, it can also do the opposite. It can make them realize that, once they've seen what lawyers actually do or what it's actually like to be inside a law firm, they have absolutely no interest in becoming a lawyer or going to law school. So they keep the vegan donuts for themselves, and leave Hemp on his own to find other edibles to help make it through the day.

Whether it confirms or destroys your original idea that law school was the place for you— either way, this is very useful information. I have had several former students who were convinced they wanted to go to law school, then took my advice and worked for a summer in a law firm and suddenly— voila!—law school no more. I'm not trying to scare anyone away from law school with this advice. Nor am I saying *everyone* should work at a law firm before even considering law school. But if you are on the fence, or there is some voice in the back of your head that keeps wondering if there is some other path that might be better for you, then by all means seek out a job in a law firm. As I said, it can either confirm that you made the right choice, or save you from the grief of making the wrong one. Just don't do it because you think it will improve your chances of getting in, because as I said, it won't. Law schools assume that everyone who shows up on the first day of the first year of law school is pretty much a blank slate, a sponge named Bob in search of oddly geometric pants. They know you want to study law, but they don't assume you know anything about it. You can't test out of courses like you could as an undergrad, so you're not going to be ahead of the game by taking a bunch of law courses or working in a law firm prior to entering law school. Do it for yourself, or for your own interests, but don't do it as a strategy to get into law school. So for now, just relax and maybe have a vegan donut or two.

CHAPTER 8

I'VE MADE MY DECISION: WHERE DO I START?

L et's say you've given everything a great deal of thought, and you've finally had that wonderful epiphany in which you realize with absolute certainty and perhaps a modicum of anxiety—you definitely want to go to law school. Hooray! And congratulations on making a decision. At this point, however, your work is hardly over, because now you will move into the next stage of preparation for your law school adventure, which is the ginormous process of getting your applications together.

There are four essential elements to a law school application, and I will go over each of them in a separate chapter. As a preview, however, the four essential things a law school will use to evaluate you to see if you are worthy of a seat in their incoming class are: (1) your GPA; (2) your letters of recommendation; (3) your LSAT score; and (4) your personal statement. Keep that in the back of your mind while I talk about a few other things you might want to do, now that you've made your decision.

The first thing you will want to do is set up a file where you can start organizing the information you will need as you start the process of getting your application together. Some people set up spreadsheets for this, but if you're not all that savvy with spreadsheet software, either use this as an opportunity to learn or else find some other method of organization. There are all sorts of apps that can help get you organized as well—just find one that works for you. The kind of information you will start collecting will be things like deadlines and due dates (for law schools, LSAT registration, etc.), potential contacts for letters of recommendation, a timeline to get your application together, and any notes you collect along the way about various programs that may be of interest to you. Again, I'll come back to a lot of these points in later chapters, but for now, you should at least get started on getting organized. You'll end up collecting a lot of information very quickly and you don't just want to throw it all in a box that says "law stuff" on it.

The most important research you will do at this point is to look up as much information you can about any law school you think you want to apply to, and even about law schools that you might never have considered previously. What you will be looking for are things like the rankings of each school, whether they have specific cut-off scores for things like the LSAT or GPA, and whether or not they have specialized programs that grab your interest, such as space law or entertainment law, and so forth. If they offer joint-degree programs (which I'll talk about later), make a note of the programs that are offered and which schools offer them. I realize at this point you might just be so exhausted from making your initial decision to go to law school that the very suggestion of considering a joint-degree might fall into the TT;CT category (Too Tired; Can't Think). But later, after you've rejuvenated with a nice spicy bowl of *bibimbap* or a properly overloaded *completo*, you might come back to the idea and reconsider. When you do, you'll be happy that you kept good notes in the course of compiling your information.

CHAPTER 9

HOW IMPORTANT IS MY GPA?

As I ease into this part of the program, let me just say up front that I really detest the way that institutions of higher learning try to break down the complexity and richness of a person's life into simplified quantitative parameters that quite often fail to convey anything meaningful about that individual or the creative potential they might offer in their chosen field of study. If I ruled the world, and unfortunately I don't (working on it, though), I'd do something to change all that. So until I can set the world right, you're going to have to accept the brutal fact that most law schools use a metric when they are wading through stacks and stacks of applications and that metric is designed to make it easier to whittle down a large stack of applications into a smaller stack. It is an absolute certainty that every application season at least one person on every admissions committee will see a 3.0 GPA and simply say "nope, not good enough for us—reject!" But it breaks my heart to know that it happens, because while it's true that a 3.0 might mean that an undergrad booked a few too many tickets on the party train express, it might also mean that a student worked two jobs to help out her or his family financially while taking care of an ailing parent or sibling. In the latter case, if a student can pull off a 3.0 with that on their plate, they pretty much have attained superhero status in my book. Unfortunately there is no superhero box to check on the law school application, though I wish there were. I mean, seriously—can you imagine the unbridled awesomeness of Deadpool as a lawyer?

Let me also say that right from the start of the application process, you need to prepare yourself for the emotional roller-coaster you are about to board. It will take an enormous amount of work to put together a stellar application, and that work can be physically exhausting and emotionally draining. Once the applications go out, you have the anxiety of waiting for replies, during which time you will second-guess yourself a million times or more—pretty much every day. If you get a rejection letter, it can be soul crushing, and it is all too easy to take a rejection letter personally. *I'm not good enough for Yale*, you might think. And yes, there are examples where that is actually the case. I'm pretty sure the applicant with the 1.1 GPA who misspelled his own name on the application won't be going to Harvard Law. *Sorry, Jawn, but your application to Harvard "Law's Cool," as you put it, didn't quite make the cut.* But in most cases, it's not as clear-cut as that. There are many, many factors that influence the decisions of admissions committees, many of which are simply beyond your control. You have to learn *not* to take it personally. It might not be that you aren't good enough for Yale. It might be that Yale isn't good enough for you. Remember that.

So, back to your GPA. Is it important? Yep, it certainly is. But you have to remember that it is also only one element out of the essential four parts to your law school application, so it may not be entirely a sink-or-swim situation. Even if you have a 4.0, you have to understand that a *lot* of law school applicants have a 4.0, so clearly admissions committees have to look at other things besides GPA to help them figure out whom to put on the short list. But sticking with the GPA itself, there are things even there that a committee may look at in determining how important your GPA is in your overall application. A 4.0 with a major in Astrophysics might be interpreted differently than a 4.0 with a major in Leisure Studies (and no, Advanced Leisure Studies doesn't sound better). Some law schools take into account things like grade inflation, which universities grapple with all the time. Most admissions committees will try to discern from your transcript whether you kept your course selections or choice of major as safe as possible (taking less-challenging classes, for instance) simply to keep your GPA high. If you did, it will count against you.

For those that double and triple majored as an undergrad, don't assume that this will automatically work in your favor or will make up for a less-than-ideal GPA. A 3.5 with a triple major is not inherently better than a 4.0 with one major. More often than not, an admissions committee will assume you probably didn't manage your studies well and therefore shouldn't have tried a triple major in the first place. There has been a growing tendency in recent years for undergrads to reach for more than one major, thinking it looks more impressive. Please, I'm begging you—do not add a major with the idea that it will help you get into law school. Add a major if you know it is what you want to do, and if you know you can handle the additional workload. Having one major and doing it well counts just as much if not more than a double or triple or quintuple major done much less well when it comes to evaluating applications.

It's true that some schools have absolute cut-offs when it comes to GPA. But there is also something else you should consider if your GPA is not what you hoped it would be as the result of what might be called exceptional circumstances. Some law schools state explicitly that you can add an addendum to your application to explain exceptional or extenuating circumstances. Other law schools don't invite such a statement, but if you feel it is warranted, add it anyway. The worst that can happen is that the law school won't look at it or consider it. But if you had a semester where things went off the rails a bit, and if it was due to exceptional circumstances beyond your control, such as a personal tragedy or a protracted illness, then why not explain the circumstances? The academic school year comes in neatly-packaged chronological segments called semesters (or quarters), whereas life is chronologically messy and unpredictable and doesn't care when finals week is. Anyone looking at your transcript would notice if you had a bad semester or two in an otherwise stellar undergrad career. If they have a better picture of why and how that happened, it might help the admissions committee make a more informed and more ethical decision about your application. Note that the key word here is *might*. If you happen to apply during a year when the admissions committee is filled with doltish curmudgeons, then they might not care about what they see as a boohoo story from one more whiny, petulant applicant. This is why I told you never to take the decisions of admissions committees personally.

CHAPTER 10

WHOM SHOULD I ASK FOR LETTERS OF RECOMMENDATION?

Letters of recommendation are the part of the application that creates the most social anxiety, because it is the only one of the four essential elements of the application that requires you to ask other people for help. On top of that, you have to rely a bit on blind trust because for the most part, you don't know what those people are going to say about you. Not to worry—there's a strategy for negotiating this part of the application, and it starts long before you ever knew you wanted to go to law school.

First, I will talk about what you want in a letter-writer. The strongest letters of recommendation are the most personal ones, letters that show a real knowledge of you and your work, so you want to ask people who know you well. You might have taken a class with a Nobel Prize-winning economist and then might have been tempted to ask her for a letter of recommendation, thinking "with a letter from her I'm sure to get in anywhere." But if the most detailed thing the Nobel Prize-winning professor can say about you is something like "Tejinder is a carbon-based life form," then that letter is all but useless for your application.

What are the most important traits and characteristics about you that a law school wants to see in your letters? First and foremost, perhaps, is that you can work well on your own. That doesn't mean you are anti-social, but what a law school doesn't want is a student that needs help every step of the way or has to ask ten thousand questions about each part of the assignment. So if you were the type of student who continually asked questions in a class like "what are you looking for in this assignment?" or "how many sources do I need?" then you probably won't want to ask that professor for a letter. A sentence like "Sergei would always approach me at the end of class and ask me to recommend sources or ask for hints on each assignment" might sound like it is describing an enthusiastic student, but what it's really doing is crushing your chances of getting into law school. A law professor wants to be able to assign a 20-page paper, due at the end of the semester, and know that you either know how to write a good 20-page paper or will figure out how to write one *on your own.*

Other traits and characteristics that are very helpful in letters are things that made you stand out in a class. Perhaps you wrote a uniquely creative paper in one class, or perhaps you took your research skills to a whole new level in another. Law schools are looking for well-rounded people, too, so if your sense of humor came through in a class and the professor picked up on it, that's the kind of information a law school admissions committee wants to know about. The same is true if you exhibited a smooth ability to work well under pressure. Law school is full of pressure, you see, and an admissions committee that sees reassurance in a letter that you can handle it well will certainly work in your favor.

So how do you make sure that all this kind of information ends up in your letters of recommendation? Well, here's where you need to strategize a bit, and do so in advance, even before you knew you wanted to go to law school. If you happen to be in a school or a department where your classes are small and have lots of time for class-based discussion, then your professors will probably get to know you personally right in the classroom. But that isn't always the case. Many schools or programs have large or very large classes, or even if they have small ones, you might be the kind of person who has a hard time speaking in class. If that is the case, then there's another option for you that you should definitely take advantage of: office hours. All professors have office hours, and for some reason, they seem to be very intimidating to students, like some sort of great mystery that students need to solve but can't. And while it's true that there are many professors who view their undergrads as idiots, infants, and imbeciles, most professors aren't like that. I for one enjoy my office hours because it gives me a chance to get to know my students on a more personal level, something I can't always do in a large lecture course.

One more point about office hours. While you can certainly go to office hours to ask questions about an assignment or a reading or a complex point brought up in lecture—the ability to work well on your own doesn't mean you *never* ask questions like that—there are other reasons to go to office hours as well. Did a particular lecture resonate with you? Follow up with a visit to office hours to let your professor know. Did the professor go over a case study that just so happens to be a place where you lived or visited? Follow up with a conversation about it in office hours. The conversations I remember most from office hours are the ones that involved conversations that were clearly based on genuine interest in my class or in class-related issues, and those are the types of conversations that allow me to add personal details to the letters of recommendation I write for my students. So please do take advantage of office hours—they're a great opportunity to expand your overall experience while at university and also a great way to make your education feel much more personal than it might otherwise be.

When it comes time to request letters of recommendation, then, you want to approach the professors that you feel know you best and in whose classes you did well. There's an unwritten ethical rule that if a professor feels she or he cannot write you a strong letter of recommendation, then they should tell you so. But that doesn't always happen. So when you approach a professor to ask for a letter of recommendation, try to gauge their reaction. If you get a response like "I'd be happy to write one for you!" then you're in good shape. If the professor starts weeping or laughing or both, or if the response is something like "sure, whatever," you might want to look elsewhere.

Not all of your letters have to be from professors. If you were on a team of some sort, athletic or otherwise, or if you did a meaningful internship where your talents really shined, or if you volunteered somewhere that reveals what motivates and inspires you, then a supervisor or coach or boss can often write a letter for you that nicely complements your academic ones.

Lastly, once you have your letter-writers lined up, get the timing right. You definitely want to ask in advance. I ask for a minimum of one-month advanced notice and quite frankly more than that is even better. If you are going to take a year off, you can ask for letters before you graduate, and either have them sent to a letter service or else get back in touch with your letter-writers again as you start putting your applications together. Remember, too, that a day in the life of a professor is insanely busy (and the nights are crazy wild), so if you send an email and don't get a response, don't feel crestfallen or rejected. Just re-send the email in a couple of weeks or so. I get well over 200 emails a day, and sometimes an email re-send is exactly what I need to re-member something that got lost in the endless obligations of the day. Persevere without being obnoxious—it's the secret of life.

CHAPTER 11

HOW SHOULD I APPROACH THE LSAT?

I f you're like most people, you'll approach the LSAT with cold sweats and nausea. No one enjoys the LSAT, and if you ever meet someone who says they did, then stay as far away from that person as possible. Something is very wrong with them. The LSAT is a bit like dental surgery, only without the anesthesia. Yep, it's a festival of pain, but there's no way around it, so you'll have to bite the bullet and get through it as best you can. One thing, though: don't bite the bullet too hard—you might need dental surgery.

Of the four essential elements in your application, the LSAT is the one that is the least forgiving. While you might be able to explain a bad semester because you were blindsided by one of those tragedies or setbacks life often dishes out with impeccably inconvenient timing, you'll have no such luck explaining a bad LSAT score. It can sink you more than any other part of the application. Law school admissions committees lean on the LSAT score pretty heavily, especially in making the first cut of applications. Law school folks continuously insist that there is a strong correlation between a student's LSAT score and their performance in law school, but I'm not convinced the correlation is based on intelligence but rather on the ability to commit an inordinate amount of time and energy to an amazingly pointless task. It's a reality you have to accept, whatever the correlation is, so what that means is you'll have to give the LSAT some respect. A stellar LSAT score (like 170) can easily offset a slightly problematic GPA, but if you blow the LSAT and bring in a score of 125 or so, your 4.0 won't help you at all and your chances of getting in plummet rapidly.

In short, you need to take the LSAT seriously. What that means is that you will have to study for it, and that brings up the question that everyone always asks about the LSAT, which is whether or not to take those LSAT prep classes. That requires me to introduce something I'll come back to a bit later that relates to the expense of law school. LSAT prep classes are generally expensive, some more than others, but you need to look at the cost of those classes as an *investment* rather than an expense. Another reason to take the LSAT prep classes, even if you think you don't need them, is so that you know what your competition knows. The LSAT is a very competitive exam, and sometimes the difference of just two points on your score can have a massive influence in terms of what percentile you fall into. Knowing what your competition knows can be a considerable asset in approaching the LSAT, and as anyone in the financial world can tell you, the acquisition of assets is always seen as an investment rather than an expense.

I'll admit, I have had students who do not take those prep classes and who do very well on the LSAT, so don't think I am telling you it's an absolute necessity. Most people take the prep classes because studying for the LSAT is like gargling with Sriracha sauce—it hurts, and appears to serve no purpose. Taking the classes gives you the kind of disciplinary nudge that many people need when it comes to the LSAT, whether it is someone to set deadlines for them, someone to put them in a windowless room for a practice LSAT session (okay, the room might have windows, but you won't be looking out them, so what's the point?), and so forth. If you think you have the kind of self-disciplined study habits it takes to stay focused on preparing for the LSAT all on your own, then by all means do so. But please do be honest with yourself on this point. I know lots of people who *claim* to be self-disciplined or who *claim* to be great at multi-tasking, but in reality most of them are self-disciplined in specifically useless skills like taking long naps or playing Candy Crush for hours on end, and the multi-taskers usually only succeed in doing many things poorly all at the same time.

While it's true you can take the LSAT more than once, it behooves you to do everything possible to nail it on the first try. Taking the LSAT twice is a bit like drinking that expired milk in your fridge with the slightly funky smell and chunky texture, getting mercilessly sick, and then when you recover, going back for another glass thinking the first one must have been a one-off thing. You should only consider retaking the LSAT if you know with absolute certainty that you will improve your score significantly. It can actually look impressive to an admissions committee if you scored a 155 (respectable) the first time around and then scored a 165 (exceptional) on the second effort. Very few people can pull of a 10-point gain in their score. But if you do the whole thing over just for an additional point or two, it really isn't worth it.

As I write this, it is slowly becoming a thing for law schools to drop the LSAT as a requirement for admission. You'll still have to take a standardized test (most likely the GRE), but law schools are slowly realizing that the LSAT is at a minimum a brain-eroding hazing ritual and at a maximum a potential violation of one or more human rights principles. There is also a bit of grumbling against the testing monopoly of the people who administer the LSAT, but there's no need to go into detail about that here. The main thing is to be on the lookout for changes in the LSAT requirement. A day in which you take the LSAT only to realize afterward that you didn't need to is a very bad day indeed.

CHAPTER 12

HOW SHOULD I WRITE MY PERSONAL STATEMENT?

The personal statement element of your application is probably the most difficult part to write. Sure, the LSAT is no word-based carnival, but there is at least a process to it that is decidedly impersonal. If you follow the necessary steps, chances are, you'll do well, even if each of those steps is on a pathway made of nails. But the personal statement is a whole different literary beast. What makes it so difficult is that it's you writing about you. It's 2-3 blank pages staring at you and asking you to write out some part of your life in just the right way so that you will appear scintillating and interesting to people who don't know anything about you, aside from your GPA and your LSAT score. It's just one part of the application, and yet suddenly you find yourself veering into unexpectedly deep questions like, "what kind of life have I lived?"

The personal statement in a law application also offers a glimpse into the differences between professional school and graduate school. When you apply to a graduate program, the essay you submit is intended to show how you think—the questions that interest you and the kinds of research you want to pursue as you begin your graduate studies. When you apply to a professional school, and of course law school is a professional school, since you'll be following roughly the same curriculum as everyone else in your cohort and it is assumed you'll develop your interests after you start law school, what admissions committee want to know is what kind of a person you are and what brought you to the decision to go to law school. Law schools go to great lengths to assemble an entering class that incorporates a wide variety of backgrounds and life experiences, and they look to the personal statements to help make this happen.

One way to approach your personal statement is to think of someone on an admissions committee who picks up your personal statement with the question: "Would I want to have coffee with this person?" The idea here is that if someone on an admissions committee ended up in a café with you, and you both sat down across from each other with your green chai tea soy decaf lattes and had a conversation, would the admissions committee member think afterward something like "wow, this has been a wonderful conversation, I'm so happy I met you!" or would they think "wow, there's ten minutes of my life I'll never get back"? And while it is certainly true that essays that talk about how surfing that first big wave at Mavericks showed Taslima that she could overcome any challenge, or about how climbing Mt. Everest in a tutu was just the right moment of empowerment that Yudianto needed, are obviously going to attract a certain amount of attention from the admissions committee, don't feel in any way that you aren't up to par if you haven't done things like win a gold medal in full-contact curling.

What you don't want to do is write an essay about how much you want to study law. If you are applying to law school, then it is already clear that you want to study law. You can also save the stories you might have about how growing up, your parents and friends always told you something like, "wow, you should be a lawyer." Not only is that a weak foundation for the decision to go to law school, but also, when people tell you "you should be a lawyer," they aren't giving you a compliment. What they are telling you is that you are argumentative about pretty much everything and it's unbelievably annoying. Admissions committees aren't looking for annoying people, though as you'll discover when get to law school, many get through anyway.

What you do want to write about are transformative moments in your life, moments that made you who you are, and perhaps, made you think about law school and all things related. Maybe you studied abroad in South Africa and learned about apartheid and it ignited a passion for justice. Or maybe you had an encounter with a refugee right in your own hometown and it changed the way you see everything. Or maybe you are a musician and learning to play the blues turned your life around and moved it in a whole new bluesy direction. It can be big things or small. It can be things that happened elsewhere or things that happened right in your own home. Law schools use the personal statement to figure out what kind of person you are, what makes you tick—what talk you talk and what walk you walk—to help determine if, in addition to the other three essential elements of your application, you're also going to be a wonderful addition to the incoming cohort of law students.

One last thing. Do feel free to be creative in your personal statement, but understand there are limits to what you can get away with. Don't write your personal statement using only emojis, for instance. While that would certainly be creative, reading even two pages of emojis is mentally draining, and emoji-crafted essays are open to wide variations in interpretation, almost none of which will work in your favor. Remember, people on admissions committees have to read through very large stacks of applications. You might write your personal statement as if it were a scene in a Quentin Tarantino movie, for example, and then marvel at your masterpiece, thinking, "this is going to blow them away!" Yet when a weary-eyed member of the admissions committee comes across your essay, they might just think, "I don't have time for this." The most original and interesting thing in your personal statement is you. Let that come through clearly, and you'll be in excellent shape.

CHAPTER 13

WHICH SCHOOLS SHOULD I APPLY TO?

The first and most important thing I'll say on this point is this: never undersell yourself. *Never.* That's as important in life as it is in law school. So many times I have heard from students applying to law school things like, "I know I won't get in at Harvard Law School so I won't even try." I'll admit there are certain circumstances in which I might gently encourage a student to consider alternatives. If you graduated from the University of Northern South Dakota with a 1.3 GPA in Basic Communications, and your letters of recommendation are from your parents, then yes, there's a pretty good chance you won't be Harvard bound. And while I understand the need to be realistic about things, especially given the fact that it costs money to apply to schools, my experience over the years has been that most students don't appreciate or realize how good they are—as people, as students, and as potential law school candidates.

Law schools are ranked and are placed in tiers. Because law school is a professional school, part of that ranking is based upon the ability of that school to place their graduates in good legal positions on a consistent basis. The higher the tier of the law school, the better chance you will have as a graduate to start your legal career in a good position. In any discussion between legal types who meet each other for the first time in a professional context, one of the first questions that will invariably come up is "Where did you do your J.D.?" It's a way of sizing each other up. The better the law school, the more clout you carry. I don't necessarily agree with it or even like it, but it shows how much importance is attached to the law school you attended.

When I was discussing the LSAT and whether you should pay the money for the LSAT prep schools, I introduced the idea of looking at the money you spend on law school as an *investment* rather than an expense. You might be tempted to economize with the law school applications, but I wouldn't recommend doing that. I do understand that not everyone has the means to fork over $1500 just for the application fees alone, so what I am getting at here is that you should do whatever is financially feasible up to the maximum amount you can possibly afford. Once you've gone through the whole exhausting process of deciding to go to law school, don't sell yourself short in the application process and don't economize on the possibilities for your future.

To offer one example of bad planning, let's take the case of Makayla, a hypothetical law school applicant whom I happen to know very well, hypothetically at least. Like far too many students, Makayla has a tendency to undersell herself, and on top of that, like far too many people, she's working long hours to make ends meet and barely gets by. She decides to play it safe, and apply to two schools, both of which are in the city where she lives. The schools aren't highly ranked, but Makayla figures that this will make the decision even safer, because she's absolutely sure at least one of them will accept her. In fact, she was only going to apply to one of them, but opted for a second application just as a fail-safe option.

Here's the thing. Makayla is actually a very talented student. The schools she applied to recognized that, and then here's the really weird part: neither accepted her. Why? Because they were certain someone with her talents would get an offer from a much higher-ranked law school and she would undoubtedly take that offer when it was made, so the two schools to which she applied figured it would be a wasted effort to make her an offer, since she would most likely be going elsewhere anyway. Admissions committees have only a limited number of seats to offer, so they have strategies of their own about how to best fill those seats. In the case of Makayla, she made what she thought was a completely safe choice, and ended up without any options. Now she has to wait a year for the next application cycle, and is also out the money she spent on her two applications.

The point is, you should make the most ambitious strategy you can in terms of (money) quantity and (school) quality. Even if you are geographically restricted—perhaps you need to care for a family member or your spouse/partner/kangaroo has a great job and cannot relocate—you can still make optimal choices. Spend whatever you can and apply to anything and everything you think is possible. The absolute worst thing a law school can do is not accept you, so you've got nothing to lose and everything to gain by making an optimal strategy.

I'll close by reminding you one more time not to take the decisions that law schools make about you personally. I know it's hard to do, but you really need to understand that there is a certain amount of randomness in the application process that is simply beyond your control. It's entirely possible, for instance, that your LSAT score and GPA were lower than another applicant's, and yet your personal statement was about how reading King Lear changed your life, and the admissions committee member who first read your application was a Shakespeare aficionado who laments how law school students don't appreciate great literature. You get an offer, which is wonderful for you, but the other student who actually scored higher gets rejected and no doubt thinks, "I wasn't good enough." Actually you were both great enough, but a random and chance occurrence created this particular outcome, and with the same two applications at a different school with a different committee, the results could easily be reversed.

CHAPTER 14

WHICH SCHOOL SHOULD I CHOOSE?

Wait, you got in? Woohoo! After months of anxious waiting, the acceptance letters have finally started arriving, and only then do you discover a whole new source for a renewed spell of anxiety: all of them seem to want to know your decision pretty quickly. At this point, you enter the next nerve-rattling stage of decision-making, which is how to figure out which *one* school you will choose to attend. That's right, after all of the things you done to get into law school up to this point, it all comes down to one choice. It's easy to second-guess yourself repeatedly—what if I make the wrong choice? The good news is that there is a considerable amount of systematic thought you can put into the decision-making process to make sure you make the optimal choice, so let's walk through a few scenarios and see how this plays out in my very real, hypothetical universe.

Let's start with the best-case scenario, one that I sometimes refer to as the "embarrassment of riches" situation. This is what happens when you get accepted to all or nearly all of the law schools to which you applied. The good news is, clearly everybody wants you. You're a hot legal commodity, and it's good to know all of your hard work has brought you to this point. It will sink in very quickly, however, just how tough of a choice this is going to be for you. I've tried not to name specific law schools throughout this most epic and awesome guide, but for the sake of example, let's say you got into ten schools and you've at least narrowed your choices down to Yale, Harvard, Stanford, and Chicago. In this scenario, you can't really make a wrong choice, because schools that are closely ranked within the same tier don't really differ all that much.

Unlike graduate school, where your decision might be made based upon whom you might want to work with in your research, law school is really about the professional doors that a particular law school will open for you. So between these four schools, they'll all open lots of doors for you, so you can look to other things to help make your decision. Perhaps there is a specific type of law you are interested in (such as maritime law) and one of those schools has a special program in that field. Or considering that they are all top schools, perhaps geographic location or weather are things to consider. Have family and friends in the Midwest? Chicago might just be the answer. As for weather, well, I once gave a talk at Harvard Law School in the month of February, and on the day my talk was scheduled, I took a look at the weather as I ate breakfast and the *high* for that day was forecast to be 0 degrees. I thought it was a typo—surely a more humane number like 4 or 5 was missing from the front of the zero. But no, zero was the high. I suppose it might arguably be a good strategy to attend law school in a place with such miserable weather, since you'd never be able to go outside and so you'd spend all your time studying inside. But just for comparison, consider that the same argument holds true for being in prison. Just saying.

The main point from the first scenario is to understand that if you have to choose from a few schools that are very similar in ranking, then any choice you make will probably be fine. I understand there are people who like cold weather, in the same way that I understand there are people who think *Twilight* is a great movie. But I also understand there are people who think California is full of earthquake-loving, more-liberal-than-thou hipster snobs, or Chicago is a place where life moves pretty fast, so if you don't stop and look around once in a while, you could miss it. In the latter case, you might consider taking a day off to take stock of things. But whatever it is that floats your legal boat or gives you any sort of preference of one over the other, your choice will for the most part be perfectly fine.

For the second scenario, let's suppose you got into a lot of schools but they're *not* all ranked closely together in the same tier. Now what should you do? The answer here is fairly straightforward: *unless you have a compelling reason to do otherwise, choose the one with the best ranking.* I do understand that for some people, it simply isn't possible to relocate to another part of the country, perhaps for family reasons or relationship reasons or simply because the idea of a place where zero degrees can be the high temperature unsettles the soul. In these situations, you still choose the highest ranked school you can within your specific constraints.

I'm not trying to be an elitist with this emphasis on higher-ranked schools, but there really is an important thing to remember when it comes to making a choice. *Where you go to law school matters.* It matters to other legal professionals and it matters to you in terms of which professional doors the school of your choice can open. Higher rankings for law schools are based heavily on placement percentage (as in, how many graduates land a good legal job after graduating). You'll be spending a lot of money for law school (see the next two chapters on that), so you will want to get the largest return possible for your investment.

And this brings me to the last scenario, which is what happens if you get accepted only to one school, and it certainly isn't your top choice. You might think that you don't have a choice—you've only got one offer, and that's the one you have to take. But that isn't necessarily the case. One thing you shouldn't do is to accept the offer and then defer for a year to try again for a better school in the next application cycle. That's unethical and unfair to the school that accepted you. You *can* decline the offer and go through the whole process all over again the following year, but I would only recommend doing that if you are quite certain you can put together a much better application in the following year. If not, accept the offer you have and then focus on how you can make the best of it.

Remember, too, that while ranking is important, it isn't everything. In many parts of the country, local loyalty is highly valued in professional communities. If you're a Texan and know you want to practice law in Texas because you've got a Texas-sized love for Texas, you'll discover that many of your professors in a Texas law school will be from Texas, as will many of the professional connections the school has in the law community in the area. This can be incredibly helpful in getting your Texan law career slid-ing into a comfy pair of Texan boots. And don't confuse law school rank with quality of law lectures, either. Top-tier law school doesn't always mean top-tier lectures. Some of the most erudite and eloquent law lectures I have ever heard were often in the most unranked of places.

CHAPTER 15

IS IT REALLY WORTH THE MONEY TO GO?

Let me tell you something you already know: law school is expensive. Top tier schools will average $50-60k per year, and even if you go the route of a state university law school and you can pay in-state tuition, you're still looking at $30-40k per year. Law books tend to be expensive, and you'll have to buy a lot of them, and with very few exceptions, you can't sell them back like you could as an undergrad. It's unlikely you'll finish law school for less than $120k, and more likely it'll be closer to the $200k mark by the time you're done. Those are pretty sobering numbers to ponder. For some, they're downright frightening. In a place like Ohio, you can buy a very nice house for $200k. So of course you are going to have moments throughout the whole law school thing when you think to yourself: is it really worth the money to go?

Here is the part of this word carnival where I really bring home the point that I made previously. You have to look at the cost of law school as an *investment*, and not as an expense. You are in essence investing in your own future. All investments carry risks, and the riskier the investment, the higher the potential pay-off. The way this plays out in law school is like this.

Suppose you are sitting in Lincoln, Nebraska, and you've got two offers from two different law schools sitting in front of you. One is from the University of Nebraska, and since you are a born-and-raised Cornhusker, you are entitled to pay in-state tuition. University of Nebraska College of Law is quite the bargain for resident Cornhuskers, and clocks in at about $15-20k per year. That's an amazing bargain. The other offer you have is from the University of Virginia, which is going to cost you close to $60k per year, but is also much higher-ranked than the University of Nebraska and in fact is considered a top-tier law school. In this situation, which one do you accept?

This is the moment when you have to prioritize investment over expense. If you look at it from an expense standpoint, the answer is obvious—University of Nebraska College of Law is clearly the better bargain. But depending on what kind of law you want to pursue, or where you want to practice law, or how you want your law career to play out, it may not be the best investment. Taking on what might be four times the debt to go to the University of Virginia might seem foolhardy and frightening, but there are good reasons to look at is as a more lucrative investment that might offer a better return in the long run.

Let me clarify here that I'm not saying that the University of Nebraska College of Law is not a good school. It's a great school, in fact, and has the distinction of being ranked as the best bargain in law school, just so you know. So it certainly isn't the case that the Criminal Procedure (Crim Pro in law-school talk) class you take at the University of Virginia will cover more material and provide better information or even have a more dynamic professor in the classroom. The Criminal Procedure class at Nebraska might be absolutely amazing, and to be fair, it's obviously going to be good if not excellent at Virginia, too.

So if the classes might be similar in quality of instruction and material covered at both universities, what justifies paying four times more for one than the other? Remember, law school is a professional school, so you aren't just paying for the educational part of the gig, you are also paying for the professional part. The professional part is where you pay for access to the connections and clout that a particular law school has built over time, connections and clout that can automatically put you at the top of the list for highly competitive positions in the world of legal professionals. If you need those connections and you need that clout to get you to where you think you want to be, then you'll have to make the necessary investment to get it.

At this point you might be thinking, then why would anyone ever go to the University of Nebraska College of Law? The arrogant answer is because they couldn't get in anywhere else, but that's both unkind and incorrect. If a person is a native Cornhusker and they know they want to stay in Nebraska, either to practice law or to get involved with state-level government and criminal justice, it would make perfect sense to go to U of N College of Law. Their networks and clout will rank very highly not only among lawmakers and legal professionals in the state, but also among clients who value local loyalty and local knowledge. There are both clients and legal professionals in Nebraska—and this is true in many states—that would simply rather work with someone whose credentials and experience are home-grown. In that case, a law degree from the University of Virginia may not be the better investment.

If, however, the potential candidate had a desire to work, say, at the federal level of government, or had a particular interest in international business law, it would make more sense to be at place like the University of Virginia, where they would have pretty much a front-row seat to that kind of legal theater and more direct connections to professional networks in both of those fields than they might have had back in Lincoln.

At the end of the day, there is something to be said for not letting cost influence your decision too much. Looking at the cost and thinking about loans creates a lot of anxiety, I know, but when you think of it as an investment rather than an expense, it casts everything in a much better light. *Law school is worth the cost*, as long as you know for sure that it is the right choice for you. In fact, if you've already made the choice to go to law school, then there's pretty much no alternative to get you to where you want to be. So do give some thought to where you think you might want to be and what you might want to do in the world of law, and then invest in yourself and invest in your future with a clear and optimistic conscience. Great things in life rarely happen without at least some risk and uncertainty involved, and law school is no exception.

CHAPTER 16

IS THERE ANY WAY TO AVOID ALL THAT DEBT?

Having just laid out with efficient brutality how much money law school will cost, let me now soften the blow a bit by telling you that there are in fact ways to make law school more affordable or to reduce the amount of debt you'll assume to get through law school. I'll break them down into three categories: before, during, and after law school.

Starting with the *before* category, the most obvious way to reduce the cost of law schools is through a scholarship. Law school scholarships are hard to come by, so if one (or more) of your chosen law schools offers you a full or partial scholarship, you're definitely doing something right. That can certainly help in the decision making process as well when it comes to choosing which law school to choose. What many prospective candidates don't know, however, is that there are other scholarships that you can apply for that are for the most part privately endowed, and some of them are pretty obscure. This is a good chance to perfect your online research skills to see what options are out there that you might be eligible for. You might come across something like The Ice Cube Society, which will pay your tuition and fees for any semester in which you study Polar Law. Or you might discover that various tech companies have scholarships for the study of tech law, cybersecurity law, and so forth. Lastly, I'll offer as a reminder that in an earlier chapter I talked about the benefits of taking time off between undergrad and law school, and mentioned that sometimes just working can be a great thing to do. It might not offset your loans, but if you start law school knowing you've got $10k in savings to fall back as a rainy day fund, it does provide a certain amount of financial comfort.

In the *during* category, aside from the possibility that you might apply for a scholarship of some sort after you start law school, there are other things you can explore, depending on the law school you are attending. One thing you should definitely look for are on-campus positions as a research assistant or a teaching assistant. Yes, this will require you to budget time to work outside of your already packed law school schedule, but there are great incentives to do so. I should also add that many of these positions can be found outside of law school, in other departments on campus. Not only can such positions give you incredible experience, but also they do make one valuable contribution toward your expenses at law school. In most universities, if you work as a teaching or research assistant, your monthly salary certainly won't be anything you can retire on, but for the semester during which you are acting as an assistant, the university will pay your tuition and fees. I love hiring law students as teaching assistants, because it's a win-win situation. I get a wonderful teaching/research assistant, and the teaching/research assistant gets a semester in which they are (mostly) debt-free. I once hired a law student for six semesters straight (he was an exceptional teaching assistant), which means he never had to pay tuition during his entire time at law school.

Finally, we get to the *after* category. While you can't retroactively apply for scholarships, of course, you can check into the many possibilities that exist whereby private or public employers will in some cases pay off your law school loans for you, in whole or in part, usually based on how long you work for them. There are other programs through which this can happen as well, depending on the type of law work you do straight out of law school. I'll cover these in more detail in a later chapter, but for now, just know that this is certainly a possibility you should explore.

Law school is expensive, but at least now you know you have a number options to make it less so. You really should cast a net far and wide in looking for possibilities to make law school less of a financial burden, although if you just decide to take out all the loans you need and not bother with it, you wouldn't be alone and in fact would be in good company. But with a little research, you will come across possibilities out there that many people don't even know exist. Very few law school candidates and students know about the FLAS fellowship, for instance. The Foreign Language and Area Studies fellowship, funded by the US government, pays your tuition and fees in full *and* provides a reasonably generous stipend, in exchange for you enrolling in a language course each semester. On top of that, there is surprisingly no obligation for you to commit to government work after you graduate. Pretty amazing, right? The language you choose has to be a "strategic" language (there is a list on the FLAS website), which often means less commonly taught but not necessarily obscure. Not all law schools can host FLAS programs, so do check into this before applying.

The point is—you have options, should you wish to pursue them. It might involve extra work, but it's all good work, and good work often leads to other good things. So in some ways, law school is a lot like love (sorry, having a Berkeley moment).

CHAPTER 17

WHAT'S THE POINT OF LAW SCHOOL?

The point of law school is to ruin your life. Haha, just kidding. Or am I? Seriously, though, law school really does have a point, and understanding that point will help you make sense of what's about to come your way. Rather than keep you waiting, I'll just spell it out for you: *the point of law school is to prepare you to take the bar exam.*

That's not the only point, but it's definitely one of the central purposes of law school. You might be thinking, "why don't I just take the bar exam then and save myself three years of school?" Well, the answer is this: the bar exam is a very difficult exam, and you'll need a solid and broad foundation in different types of law to have any chance of passing it. I'll talk about the bar exam in more detail later, but for now, just understand that this is one of the primary purposes of law school.

The reason you should understand this little tidbit of information is because it will help you understand the structure of the law school curriculum. The law that gets taught in law school is for the most part domestic (as in, United States) law. There are other options, and I'll talk about them in a later chapter, but for the most part, the vast majority of the curriculum offered at law school is about domestic law. While you'll have a bit of choice in what you take during your first year, for the most part the first year of law school is a very intense crash course in all of the essential fields of law (civil, criminal, etc.) that you would need to know to do well on the bar exam.

The other main purpose of law school is of course to help you get a job. Not just any job—a job that relates to law and hopefully one that launches you on a good trajectory in your specific area of legal interest. For almost all legal careers, you'll have to take the bar exam to practice, so the preparation for the bar exam is also the preparation to establish a career. But there's more to it than that, and this is where the part about law school rank and reputation come into play. One of the things you are paying for, or one of the things you are *investing in*, when you choose a law school, is the vast network of connections that the law school has built over the years with persons in all areas of legal practice. Law, like so many other professions, is an occupation that thrives on connections, not in a shady, corrupt sort of way, but in a standard, professional sort of way. Since law schools are ranked partly on their ability to land you a good legal job right out of law school, it means they need to have a good network to connect you with in order to make that happen. Legal networks open legal doors for you.

Lastly, the point of law school isn't just to allow you access to pre-existing networks of legal professionals. The other side to this in law school—and this is why law schools put so much care into assembling the best entering cohort they can—is to create an incoming class that establishes a bond during their three yeas of law school so that they will eventually become part of the well-connected network of alumni that future law students can rely upon. This is why you'll discover once you get to law school that there are a surprising number of social events and mixers that are hosted by the law school itself. The studying and socializing are *both* essential parts of your time in law school. Oh, and if you're thinking that you're amazingly awesome in your social media skills, and so you can skip the socializing and just network online, you should know that law is still a profession that values personal, face-to-face interaction far more than online emoji-fests or tweet-sized comments.

And on that note, once you start law school, be cautious about what you post on social media. You're in a professional school now, which means you're expected to start acting like a professional, too. So if you're still thinking of getting that gnarly tattoo of Hello Kitty that says "I luv u 4ever," just make sure it's on your ass where no one can see it, and for the love of humanity do *not* post a picture of it on LinkedIn.

CHAPTER 18

SHOULD I CONSIDER A JOINT DEGREE?

If you're the kind of person who likes to run a triathlon while brushing up on your language skills by listening to an audiobook on *Conversational Amharic*, then you might just be a good candidate for a joint degree program at law school. Many law school applicants don't know about joint degree programs, or find out about them only after it's too late, so I'm here to tell you what they are and what options are available to you.

The first thing I should say right from the start is that a joint degree program is not like a double major in under-grad. It's actually a separate and additional degree that you do simultaneously with your law studies, so when you finish you will have two degrees instead of one. Before you get two excited about that (get it? "two excited"...heehee), you should understand that it is therefore also twice the work. And if you think this means it will open twice as many doors for you or give you twice the salary you might otherwise get, the truth is it won't do either of those things for you. A joint degree program does offer certain benefits, however, and if those benefits translate into strong assets for your growing professional portfolio, then there are good reasons for you to consider a joint degree program.

While there are a few law schools that will allow you to submit one application for a pre-packaged joint degree program, the vast majority of joint degree programs work like this. First, you go through all the things we have already discussed to get into law school—apply, choose, and then show up. Next, in your first semester of law school, you will then submit a separate application for the second degree program of your choice, keeping in mind you'll have to do all the necessary prerequisites and requirements for that application as well (so if they want the GRE rather than the LSAT, you get to take the GRE—woohoo!). Even though there's no guarantee you'll be accepted to the second degree program, your chances of getting in are very good because (1) you're already there at the university and will be for at least for another two years, and (2) you've already been accepted to the university's law school which means you've proven yourself worthy of the official "smart cookie" designation that admissions committees look for. If you are accepted into the second degree program, you begin the coursework for the second degree during your second year of law school. Time gets condensed a little in these programs, so there is a strong incentive to do this as a joint degree rather than finish law school first and then do a second degree afterward. Law school is three years, and most other professional programs are two years. That would normally be five years of school time, but as a joint degree program, you get both degrees in four years. You've basically turned five years into four without the usual risk of needing to be near a black hole to make that happen—not even Stephen Hawking or Neil deGrasse Tyson can pull that off, though I'm sure at parties they often claim they can.

So, what kinds of options might you have? Well, standard joint degree programs are things like public policy (MPP), business (MBA), public health (MPH), and even social work (MSW). Not every law school offers joint degree programs, and those that do have different combinations to choose from. UC Berkeley for instance has a joint degree with City and Regional Planning (MCP), something that is not usually on the menu at the great food truck of law school. Wherever you end up going to law school, you will want to look into joint degree programs and do some research on them before you arrive for your first year. Things move quickly in law school, so if you're even considering a joint degree, you'll want to do as much prep work as possible *before* you arrive for that first day of law school.

Why would anyone want to do a joint degree? You should definitely not pursue a joint degree thinking it simply looks more impressive on your resume or will make you more attractive to potential employers. Like I said, it's not like a double major in undergrad, and if you put in the energy for a second degree that you clearly didn't need, it can look like you wasted time or lacked focus. Having said that, where a joint degree can be a considerable asset is when the second degree enhances your qualifications for the type of law you wish to pursue. If you wanted to pursue business law or corporate law, having a JD plus an MBA shows a potential employer that you have a special set of professional skills that other candidates might not have. The same is true if you wanted to pursue health law or even medical law and earned an MPH in addition to your JD, or if you wanted to pursue family law and had an MSW plus a JD. You get the idea.

The main thing to keep in mind is that it *can* be a very powerful addition to your professional credentials, but only if it makes sense in the context of the type of law you intend to practice. What this means is that you'll need to have some idea of what type of law you want to practice *before* you arrive at law school, since as I said, you will apply for the second degree in your first semester of law school. If you apply to an MSW program and then realize in your second year you want to focus on corporate law, then that MSW, while it might be interesting, isn't going to be a professional asset for you. Most law school students, by the way, don't pursue a joint degree, so don't feel any pressure to do so, like it's automatically the right thing to do. The JD by itself is a very powerful degree, and if it's all you need to get you where you want to be, why spend the extra time and effort getting a degree you don't really need?

So just be aware that joint degree programs exist and know that they *can* be a great set of credentials for your professional portfolio, but only if the joint degree makes sense in your professional pursuits. As with law school, first consider everything and considerate it wisely, and then make the most well-informed choice you can.

CHAPTER 19

WHAT KINDS OF LAW WILL I STUDY?

While you will have at least some choice in the types of law you study in law school, one way to look at the curriculum is to divide it into two categories, drawn in this case from the fashion industry: *essentials* and *accessories*. You could of course use the standard language of requirements and electives, but that would just be daft, and I don't mean the punk kind, so let's have some fun and turn law school into a wardrobe. Essentials refers to the classes that pretty much everyone has to take since they are considered foundational, and accessories refers to the classes that are not foundational but are directly relevant to your area of interest in the practice of law. Let's start with the essentials.

You'll meet most of the *essentials* in your first year of law school. You'll have some choice in what you take, but it's not a massive amount of choice. It's not for nothing that many first-year law students refer to the first year as boot camp. Just as anyone, even those who claim to hate fashion, has to have a collection of essential articles of clothing—underwear, socks, pants, shirts—so, too, are there essential kinds of information that every lawyer, regardless of the type of law they practice, has to have. These would include things like constitutional law (con law), criminal law (crim law), civil law (civ law), torts, criminal procedure (crim pro), civil procedure (civ pro), contracts, corporate law, family law, estate law, and property law. As I said, you'll have some choice in the ones you take, but most of them are indispensible and will definitely be on the bar exam. Things that won't be on the bar exam but are still considered essential are things like legal research and legal writing.

The *accessories* are all the classes that you take either because they are directly relevant to the kind of law you want to practice or because you just find them inherently interesting. Your schedule gets more flexible with each year of law school, so you'll most likely start choosing accessories (you can call them electives *if you must*) in your second year and third year.

The *first layer* of accessories consists of courses that are important but not generally essential. This category would include things like immigration law, income tax law, administrative law, cyberlaw, or more specialized coverage of something from an essential field, for example an entire course devoted only to the First Amendment. A class on immigration law would be essential to someone wanting to be an immigration lawyer, but not to someone who wanted to focus on corporate law (unless a corporation wanted a lawyer who could help negotiate the complex visa requirements for foreign workers). A person intending to pursue corporate law, on the other hand, should certainly consider things like income tax law, administrative law, or even cyberlaw as essential or near-essential. Accessories help you define your area of specialization, which usually starts, as I have hinted, toward the end of your first year and the start of your second year.

The *second layer* of accessories consists of courses that are either highly-specialized or else are just generally interesting. Not every law school will offer these classes, so if you know you have an interest in any of these things before you start law school, it would be a good idea to look at the course offerings and areas of specialization of some of the faculty to make sure it is an option you can pursue. This category might include things like entertainment law, which is in some ways a specialized version of contracts (when a music label "signs a band," they're signing a contract), but goes far beyond that as well. There's even a field called art law, which gets into all sorts of things about intellectual property rights, forgeries, underground art markets, and many other amazing things. Another field that used to be considered "out there" but is now becoming more mainstream and of direct relevance to many fundamental legal questions is animal law.

Tangent alert!

I know you're sitting there thinking, wait, how could animal law have any relevance to fundamental questions of law? I couldn't just leave you scratching your head in dismay and disbelief over that one, so let me explain this a bit further. Let's take what is perhaps the most fundamental legal category of all, which is personhood. I know, I know, you're about to say that we're all just people so why do we need a special legal category. Well, it turns out in the world of law not all people are persons, and some things that aren't people at all are a person, or at least a kind of one. A person is someone that can be both the subject and the object of a legal proceeding—in more colloquial terms, someone who can both sue and be sued. Children, for instance, are people but they're not persons. That 's where we get the phrase "parent or legal guardian," who are the legal persons that connect non-person children to the legal world. People who are persons are called *natural persons*. So is there an unnatural person? No one uses that name, but for purposes of law, for instance, a corporation is considered a *juridical person*, a legal construct that gives unity of action to what is essentially a large, complex, administrative entity.

So, what's the role of animal law here? Well, here's where things get fun and interesting. There have been a growing number of efforts, not just in the United States, to grant personhood to nonhuman species. You might be thinking this *has* to be some crazy California thing, a bunch of granola-eating, militant-but-nonviolent vegans who have spent way too much time inhaling the pungent herbal fog that often mists through the San Francisco Bay Area. But no, it's a very serious and fundamental challenge to the legal category of personhood, and trying to prove that an animal cannot be a legal person is much harder to do than you might think. The species boundary is becoming more and more porous every day, thanks to both legal and scientific research. And if you still think it's just a crazy idea, you should know that New Zealand—which incidentally was also the first country to extend human rights and thus personhood to some nonhuman species in 2000—became the first county in the world to grant legal personhood *to a river* in March 2017, giving the Whanganui River the same legal status as you and me. So if a river can be a person, why can't an animal be one, too? Think about it.

Here ends the tangent.

⚊╪╪⚊

The *third layer* of accessories consists of those courses that cover areas of law that are not domestic. That would be the various branches of international law, which many law students don't even bother with. International law is not something that is covered on the bar exam, and for many a law student, it remains something of a mystery. For that reason, I thought I'd spend a few chapters going over what international law is and why it might be more relevant to your area of interest than you might think. The next three chapters will go over human rights law, international law in general, and comparative law. They are extraordinarily interesting subjects to study for many reasons, not the least of which is that they operate so very differently from the way US domestic law works. So, see you in the next chapter, where a human writes about human rights.

CHAPTER 20

WHAT ABOUT HUMAN RIGHTS LAW?

Human rights are usually the first thing to come to mind for anyone who wants to fight for justice, so it might have come as a surprise to many when I didn't list it as an essential class for law school. Even more surprising is the fact that if you want to study human rights in law school, you'll have to seek it out on your own. That's because what we commonly refer to as human rights is more formally known as human rights law, and human rights law is in fact one of the branches of international law. Since international law is not a primary focus of law school, you'll have to actively and intentionally seek it out and incorporate it into your own legal curriculum.

What is perhaps most confusing for students who are new to international human rights law is that even though it is formally a part of international law, the vast majority of human rights cases are domestic cases. The reason for this legal peculiarity is that the treaties that generate human rights law are multilateral international treaties (called covenants or conventions), and nations that sign on to and ratify these treaties are in effect promising to implement and enforce those human rights principles into their domestic legal systems. There are some instances where human rights cases end up in what are considered international courts, but for the most part, as I said, human rights cases are domestic cases.

There are parts of human rights work that are considered truly international, though these parts are usually less case-specific and more institutionally focused in their efforts. These would consist of things like helping to draft new treaties, or writing reports (official or unofficial) that can assist various human rights components of international institutions in their work. At the United Nations, for example, every member country comes up for what is called Universal Periodic Review on a regular interval, during which time human rights issues and concerns are investigated to see if the country under review is improving or regressing in their human rights compliance. Human rights experts often provide information to the United Nations to assist in these reviews, especially if there are specific types of cases or concerns that they want the UN to know about in relation to a specific country. The United Nations isn't the only international institution where this type of activity occurs, so there are many institutions around the world where the work of human rights legal experts is of crucial importance.

It isn't just official organizations like the UN or the African Union that utilize the knowledge and investigative skills of human rights legal experts. There are of course non-governmental organizations (NGOs) that rely very heavily on persons trained in the intricacies of human rights law. Obviously groups like Human Rights Watch and Amnesty International put human rights work front and center in their various projects and campaigns, but so do less-well-known organizations and campaigns, such as Not for Sale (combating child sex trafficking) or local NGOs working on specific issues such as acid attacks in Cambodia or dowry deaths in India. And please don't think of human rights work as something that is only a concern elsewhere in the world. There are human rights issues and problems in *every* country in the world, including the United States.

One person who has certainly done quite a bit to raise the profile of human rights legal work in the world is human rights lawyer Amal Clooney. Yes, she's married to George Clooney, but don't think for a moment that's what gave her notoriety in the field of human rights. She was known in legal circles far before George came along and she had already earned a reputation as a formidable force in human rights work. As an example of the kind of thing a human rights lawyer might do, Amal Clooney has been, among other things, the defense counsel for Mohamed Nasheed, former president of the Maldives, in his case against the government of the Maldives. Nasheed was ousted as president in February 2012 through a series of political maneuvers that amounted to an indirect coup, or at least a form of regime change under duress. Three years later, in March 2015, he was convicted and sentenced to 13 years in prison under charges that appeared to be politically motivated rather than legally substantiated. His case was a domestic case in Maldivian courts (remember, most human rights cases are), and because the charges against him were considered more political than legal, Nasheed was considered a political prisoner, which put his case firmly within the reach of human rights law. That's how he ended up with a human rights lawyer as his defense counsel.

If human rights work sounds like the sort of thing you might want to do, then what can you do in law school to make that happen? The first thing you should do is to look into which law schools have strong human rights programs and make sure you apply to at least a few of them. UC Berkeley's California School of Law (formerly Boalt Hall), for instance, has a very well-known Human Rights Center, headed by Eric Stover, and also offers what is called a human rights clinic which gives law students hands-on experience with actual clients in ongoing human rights cases and investigations. Other law schools, such as Harvard, Columbia, and Stanford, among many others, have strong human rights programs as well, so you'll want to do some preliminary research before you apply. Once you start law school, find out what is being offered in terms of human rights law and how you can get involved in human rights as a law student. Again, you'll have to put in the effort on your own because as I said, international law (including human rights law) is not always seen as part of the central curriculum of law schools in the United States. It won't take too much effort, and if you think human rights is your thing, it is definitely worth the extra effort.

One last thing I should mention, and it is a very serious one, is that if you are thinking of getting involved in human rights law and human rights work, you will need to either have or find a deep reserve of emotional grit. When you start reading human rights cases and human rights documents, you will quickly learn of the many horrible things that human beings will do to other human beings, and immersing yourself deeply in this type of information can take you to an emotionally dark place very quickly. I teach a course on human rights law and am constantly checking in with my students about their emotional well-being. Human rights work is great work, but it exacts a very large emotional toll among its practitioners and advocates. If you go this route (and thank you for doing so if you do), be prepared for this and remember to take care of yourself. Remember also that taking care of yourself in this context is not a selfish thing. When you work in the field of human rights, your clients will need your help, and you need to be there for them when they do. Sometimes their lives will depend upon it.

CHAPTER 21

WHAT ABOUT INTERNATIONAL LAW?

International law is a bit off to the side of the yellow brick road that leads to legal wizardry. Part of the reason for this is that international law isn't going to be on the bar exam, so it certainly doesn't fall into the essentials category I talked about earlier. It's also off to the side because international law is a bit weird. Not flying monkeys weird, but weird as in—if a lion could master English, what was Toto's problem? Toto just *had* to be different. International law is a lot like Toto.

There are even those in the legal profession who don't consider international law to be law at all. That's because legal systems are supposed to have enforcement mechanisms for infractions and violations of the law, and international law seems to lack those in a very distinct way. In domestic law, if you get caught stealing something, you get arrested, prosecuted, and then, if convicted, you go to jail. In international law, if you get caught stealing something, you can choose not to recognize the jurisdiction of the court, or you can ignore the court's ruling, though if you do, other countries might try to make you feel real bad for what you've done, or they might even decide not to trade with you anymore. Clearly, you don't have those options and outcomes in domestic law. In domestic law, if you tell the judge you don't recognize the jurisdiction of the court, the court will assume that you have a problem with reality, or that you are from Berkeley. Those two possibilities are not necessarily mutually exclusive, either.

The weirdness of international law, however, is exactly what makes it so interesting. I think it is incorrect to view international law as somehow "not law" because it doesn't have the same enforcement mechanisms as domestic law. Instead, what international law has are different enforcement mechanisms, as opposed to having none at all. These take time to understand, and in spite of the criticisms of some legal experts against international law, there's no denying that it is of fundamental importance in so many areas of global activity, including things like international trade, climate change, space exploration, environmental protection (including endangered species), international diplomacy, war and peace, and terrorism. We ignore international law to our peril, so if you think you might be interested, go ahead and take the plunge. You definitely won't be in Kansas anymore (unless you are attending the University of Kansas School of Law), and studying international law won't push you off course for your standard, yellow brick road law school trajectory. The truth is, even if you decide not to pursue international law, taking a class on the topic can help you appreciate how different legal systems work (or don't), and can even help you approach domestic legal issues with a more creative perspective. It's also possible that if you listen closely to the words of the Wizard (that would be me), you might realize that the yellow brick road is simply a place where the dogs of society howl, and so you finally decide your future lies beyond the yellow brick road (if you don't get that reference, just ask any howling old owl or horny back toad).

International law is the comprehensive term for what is in fact a panoply of different branches of the same tree. I have already discussed one of those branches, which was international human rights law. So what other branches are out there swaying in the international legal wind? For starters, there's international economic law, which would include international trade and investment, international business and corporate law, and related things like international corruption and money laundering. The World Trade Organization (WTO) has its own charter (a document spelling out the legal rules and procedure of the institution) and its own dispute settlement mechanism (something like a court), both of which are integral to the field of international economic law. And don't think you'd have to work at the UN or the WTO to be an international economic lawyer. There are plenty or private law firms that specialize in this branch of international law.

There's also treaty law, which is far more important than you might think, considering treaties are the legal glue that hold the world together. If you are read in the news about a request to extradite a person from one country to another, that extradition process must be delineated in a bilateral extradition treaty. Related to treaty law would be diplomatic law, which would cover things like diplomatic immunity or the rules regarding the inviolability of an embassy or consulate. What happens, for instance, if a diplomat goes to a party, gets traumatically turnt (aka, dramatically drunk), and then causes a fatal accident on the way home? Is that action still protected by diplomatic immunity? For the answer, we have to turn to international law.

(The answer to the last question, by the way, is that the home country of the diplomat can assert that diplomatic immunity does indeed apply to the diplomat in question, and so the host country therefore cannot arrest or prosecute the diplomat, though they can expel them. The host country can also request a waiver of immunity, which, if granted by the home country, will override diplomatic immunity and allow the host country to proceed with arrest and prosecution.)

International humanitarian law (IHL) is a comprehensive term for what are sometimes referred to as the laws of war. Here the central documents are the Geneva Conventions (1949), which consist of four multilateral treaties that are monitored for the UN by the International Committee of the Red Cross (ICRC), with the help of many other organizations as well. (Just so you know, you can download the Geneva Conventions as an app.) The Geneva Conventions are used to determine, for instance, whether a war crime has occurred, at which point another branch of international law comes into play, namely international criminal law. The International Criminal Court (ICC) is a permanent court that has jurisdiction over war crimes (and other things), but the ICC, contrary to popular, legally-misinformed belief, is not a part of the UN system so not every country has joined (including the United States). If you can't use the ICC, then a whole other international legal debate ensues over which country or court can claim jurisdiction. And if you're wondering about nuclear proliferation and things like the Nonproliferation Treaty or the Comprehensive Test Ban Treaty, those are technically part of international treaty law as opposed to international humanitarian law. The same is true with the Chemical Weapons Treaty, although the use of chemical weapons in any capacity is a war crime and so that brings the possibility of international humanitarian law back into play.

Then there's a whole separate branch of law devoted to outer space, and another separate branch devoted to the polar regions of earth, though the northern and southern polar regions each have very different, separate legal frameworks (the northern polar region uses polar bears as enforcement agents, for example, while the southern region uses penguins, which is why the south is so much more chill than the north, though they don't have Netflix). There's international environmental law, which covers everything from climate change to environmental disasters to wildlife poaching to transboundary pollution issues. International maritime law might sound like it's set aside for sailors and Captain Ahab, but since international maritime law is the branch of international law that determines territorial waters and boundaries, it is of central importance in territorial disputes and boundary disputes (for instance, the current Spratly Islands Dispute).

My point here is to urge you to put international law on your law school radar screen. Lots of students ignore it, either because it isn't going to be on the bar exam or because they can't see how it's relevant for their field of specialization. But there is something empowering about understanding how the world legally holds together or legally falls apart, and something inherently interesting in it, too. And to make the point again, even if you don't work in international law, knowing how a different legal system operates can give you new insights into the workings of domestic law, something that might work to your advantage regardless of which type of legal career you pursue.

Lastly, if by chance you do decide to pursue international law, please don't think your only option is to work for the UN. The US State Department needs international legal experts, as do security consulting firms, who lean on the knowledge of international legal experts frequently. There's private international law and public international law, too, so you've got a wide variety of options to pursue if this branch of law is of interest to you. If none of this floats your boat, then no worries—provided your boat isn't violating international maritime law—but at least now you know a little bit more of what international law is all about.

CHAPTER 22

WHAT ABOUT COMPARATIVE LAW?

I n one sense, comparative law is also international law, but in another, it's something else entirely. Whereas international law proper is the law that functions at the international level, legally connecting states to one other and to international institutions, comparative law is, as its name suggests, the comparative study of different legal traditions and different domestic legal systems around the world. As with international law, it's a bit off the beaten track of the regular law school curriculum, but once again I would recommend that you consider taking the slight detour that leads to comparative law. Aside from being endlessly interesting, it can also be a valuable asset to have in your legal portfolio, for a number of reasons.

One reason it could be an asset is sheer pragmatism. Suppose there's a start-up tech company in San Francisco that has finally realized the cost of living simply makes it way too expensive to succeed or prosper in the Bay Area, so they decide to try elsewhere. Bali is just one of the many places trying to become an Asian tech hub, and so the company is thinking they'll give Bali a try. But business law and property law and contract law all work very differently in Bali than they do in the US, so what they need in that moment is someone who is an expert in Indonesian law (Bali is a part of Indonesia) to help guide them through the process and make sure they're legally on solid ground. That someone could be you.

It isn't just the American legal system that has its own specialized legal language. All legal systems have a specialized language. What that means for someone in comparative law is that you'll most likely need to learn a new language and then learn the specialized legal language of that language. This is what makes a person who knows another legal system such a valuable asset. Going back to our example of the tech start-up relocating to Bali, if you're thinking that you could see yourself in that role, then it means you'll need to start taking classes in bahasa Indonesia right away, and if you really want to take it to the next level, basa Bali as well (*bahasa* means language In Indonesian, *basa* means the same in Balinese, just so you know).

For more obvious reasons, experts in Chinese law are in very high demand (which means you'll need to know Mandarin), but there is really a need for experts in all other legal systems, so in this case just follow your interests. I once wrote a rather lengthy article on North Korea's legal system, simply because during a trip there I managed to get my hands on a sizeable collection of legal documents that weren't available outside of North Korea. I translated the documents and then used them as primary sources for the article, offering what I hoped would be useful information for anyone working on North Korean issues. That's not a plug for my own work, but rather a personal example of what comparative legal research might look like.

Even if you are thinking that you'll focus on Ireland or the UK or New Zealand, don't be fooled into thinking that just because you already know English, no translation is required. The legal language and legal procedures of most other English-speaking countries are very different from those in the US, so you'll still have to do a bit of legal translation work if you end up with American clients who want to build a school in New Zealand to teach Hobbits how to zorb.

As a reminder, in an earlier chapter I mentioned the Foreign Language Area Studies (FLAS) fellowship, sponsored by the US State Department, as a way of helping to fund law school. When you read that earlier you might have been thinking, *why would I study a language in law school?* One obvious answer to that is comparative law—that's why. You can't become an expert in Russian law without knowing Russian, and Russian is always on the list of strategic languages for the US State Department, and so this would be the perfect reason to apply for a FLAS fellowship. You say Russian, I say *pozhalujsta.*

The second reason that comparative law can be a considerable asset is a bit more conceptual but every bit as important as the first reason (which to remind you was sheer pragmatism). Different legal systems don't just have their own specialized languages when it comes to law. They also have different ways of approaching the law and different ways of understanding legal concepts. You might think theft is theft, but there are a surprisingly large number of ways to interpret theft. That won't show up in the language of the law—it shows up in the unwritten rules of legal culture. The French interpretation of what is often called a "crime of passion," for example, is extraordinarily different from the way a similar event would be approached in an American courtroom. From 1810, when the law was drafted as part of the Napoleonic Code, until 1975, when the law was finally abolished in France, it was legally permissible for a husband to kill both his wife and her lover if he caught them "in the act" (*in flagrante delicto* is the actual phrase). Though the law has been repealed, the idea that emotion should be taken into consideration for the culpability of certain crimes lives on, and remains much more influential in France and other countries influenced by the Napoleonic Code than it is in America.

Another area of comparative law where specialized knowledge would be valuable in a number of fields, far beyond law, is Islamic law. Knowledge of Arabic would be essential, of course, in order to read the appropriate texts, but it would not be sufficient. There is a very rich and long tradition of Islamic jurisprudence, with four major schools of legal thought that differ from one another in significant ways. A thorough knowledge of that jurisprudence, and a thorough knowledge of the elements of *sharia* law, which includes both civil and criminal law, would require you to go far beyond the texts themselves and into a world of concepts and practices that only years of experience can provide. While it is certainly true that *sharia* law is mostly discussed in the United States in relation to terrorism or the Islamic State—and we do need legal experts to engage with those issues as well—*sharia* law for the most part covers everyday things like marriage, divorce, adoption, inheritance, and so on. Lastly, if you are thinking of going into business law and are thinking there couldn't possibly be a reason for you to learn about Islamic law, then you should understand that there is a whole separate set of financial practices and regulations that apply in the world of Islamic banking. If an American bank wants to open a branch in a place like Kuala Lumpur (Malaysia) and wants to offer customers the option of opening an account governed by the practices and rules of Islamic banking, then anyone with a knowledge of American law, Malaysian law, and Islamic law is going to be one *very* valuable person to have on board.

The third and last reason why comparative law could be a valuable asset in law school is because of the insights it can give you about the American legal system. Just as learning a different language helps you understand your native language so much more and so much better, so too does studying other legal systems give you a whole new perspective on American legal practice. That new perspective can sometimes encourage you to think a bit outside the box, or to see opportunities where no one else can see them. These are the kind of qualities that separate good lawyers from great ones.

Comparative law also makes you more interesting at parties and a great person to have on a team for any game involving legal trivia. Knowing the general differences between civil law and common law is a great way to impress people in social venues anywhere in the world, and as for legal trivia, well, here's a freebie for you. The American legal system is based on English common law, although we've pretty much gone our own way and so the resemblance between UK law and American law is only faint at this point. Federal law in the US and the State law of forty-nine states are all based on common law, but one and only one is based on civil law (which draws heavily, by the way, from the Napoleonic Code). Who's the solitary outlier in the American system? Louisiana, that's who. Remember that when you get arrested in New Orleans for bringing your companion iguana to the *Mardi Gras* parade (it's against the law in New Orleans to bring reptiles within 200 yards of a parade).

CHAPTER 23

WHAT'S LAW SCHOOL LIKE?
THE FIRST YEAR (1L)

Ah, to be a 1L. The first year of law school will be as exciting as it will be challenging, and you should take a moment before everything starts to get crazy simply to appreciate how far you've come and what you've accomplished. You can revel in the thrill of that first week of lectures—omg, I'm finally here!—but then you'll very quickly realize just how many things have been piled on your law school plate. Law school is partly designed to teach you law, and partly designed to make sure you have no free time ever again. What I'm going to do now is walk you through the kinds of things you might expect in a typical first year of law school. Then I'm going to talk about something they don't tell you about in the anodyne official guides and sanguine welcome kits that are offered to you, which is how the first year of law school can be absolutely soul-crushing if you're not prepared for it.

The reason that the first year of law school is often referred to as "boot camp" is because it really is like basic (legal) training. You'll most likely take four courses each semester, and while you'll have a bit of choice in what you take, for the most part they will all be essential and foundational courses—the classes you will build on in later years. You'll probably be assigned to or else join a study group, and you will quickly learn how to outline cases, since that is the key to learning how law works. Outlining cases means learning how to present the facts of a case in a clear, concise manner, to specify the key legal principle(s) involved, and then to understand the holding (ruling) and the legal reasoning of the case. You will do this week after week, case after case. You can also buy pre-packaged outlines, but outlining is a good skill to develop quickly on your own.

You'll discover very quickly that law texts are, for the most part, expensive and heavy. After you recover from seeing the cost of the books you'll need for your first semester, you'll do one of two things: (1) purchase a backpack *with wheels* so you can avoid damaging your spine, back, neck, shoulders, and legs with a 175-pound burden of knowledge on your back, or (2) buy an X-Acto knife or a razor blade and start slicing pages out of your books so you can carry around only what is necessary for that week. This is slowly changing as things go digital but you'll soon discover that for the most part law is a relatively traditional field and still shows a strong preference for the printed word.

Most law schools still rely upon the so-called Socratic method of teaching, which means your courses will be taught in ancient Greek and your professor will wear a himation and eat olives. Or…maybe not. So what *is* the Socratic method? The Socratic method is a sort of question-based dialog which either challenges assertions and premises until they break down (or end in contradictions) or else leads to the most logical conclusion, which turns out to be the most convincing answer. Note that I said "the most convincing answer" and not "the truth." You will learn very quickly in law school that law and justice are less about truth than they are about persuasion. That's not because lawyers are a bunch of liars who don't care about the truth. Far from it. It's because we often have to seek justice with imperfect or incomplete knowledge, in which case we search for the most persuasive and compelling narrative that makes the best sense and produces the best justice we can hope for. Even when we have all the information, all the facts, so to speak, the law is sometimes quite complex and difficult to apply. It isn't always as straightforward as you might think to get to justice.

I mentioned that the Socratic method is a sort of dialog, so at this point you might be wondering who's included in that dialog. Well, one interlocutor will always be the professor, and the other might be…you. It depends. Because law classes in the first year tend to be large, there will be at least one week and possibly two or three in which you are "on," meaning the professor can ask you anything about any of the cases and readings that are on the syllabus for that week. You're expected to be able to reply in a well-informed, thoughtful manner, and when challenged, to be able to hold your ground. Don't be surprised if you end up with a seating chart in your law classes in the first year. This is how the professor knows who you are and knows whom to call on when it's your turn to be "on." It's also helpful because if you make an amazing insight or comment during class, or ask a particularly profound question, especially during weeks you are *not* on, then the professor has a way to know who you are.

I may have joked about law classes being taught in ancient Greek, but you will discover very quickly that the law still relies very heavily on another so-called classical language, namely Latin. Simply put, the law is full of Latin words and phrases. If you were cool like me and took Latin in high school, you'll be way ahead of the game. If you took something like French or Japanese or any other "living" language, you'll be out of luck. If that's the case then you'll get to buy a law dictionary to help you memorize phrases like *uti possidetis* or *opinion juris* or *amicus curiae*, even if you have no idea how to pronounce them or what they literally mean. I told you law school would be fun, right?

Most first year classes have one big written exam that comes at the end of the semester. Remember when you were an undergrad and you had four weeks to write a five-page paper and then you asked for an extension because you just ran out of time? Law school isn't like that. Law school does things like give you a 24-hour 20-page take home final exam. That means you pick up the question from the exam office (most law schools grade by ID numbers rather than by name, to avoid grading bias), they make a note of the time you picked it up, and by the same time the next day, you turn in a 20-page paper that offers a persuasive argument answering the question, based on everything you learned during the entire semester. Need an extension? That's easy—in law school, it's called an F.

Some time toward the end of your first semester, or perhaps at the start of your second semester, you'll start getting information about internships for the summer. What—did you think you were going to take it easy all summer? No way, my legal friend, you're in professional school now, so summer means work time, not play time. The good news is that internships in law school are often paid positions (and when they aren't the law school often provides stipends), so the days of working for free as an undergrad (a practice I detest by the way—everyone should get paid for the work they do) are behind you. This first internship is *very* important, as it can be a career-defining moment for you. If you think you want to be an international human rights lawyer, then landing an internship at the International Criminal Court would be a tremendous boost for you. If you think you want to be a corporate lawyer focusing on tech companies, an internship at Google or Facebook would give you a very large legal foot in the door. This is where the rank and status of your law school can again make a huge difference for you. Remember, you're not just paying for the education itself, you're paying for the networks that the law school has developed over the years. Those networks are what help you land the most prestigious internships.

One other fun-filled part of your time as a 1L will consist of something known as *moot court*. Moot court is your first real chance to argue a case before a panel of judges, and even though it's an artificial setting in that the case and your clients aren't real, there's a very good chance that you'll be arguing your case in front of a panel of real judges. That's because judges (acting or retired) and other members of the legal community love to offer their time to sit on the panel for moot court. Like most law courses, your grade for the semester all comes down to the one moment where you argue your case (and submit your legal brief), so the anxiety in the air is as dense as the prose of a legal textbook. If you don't have a nice professional suit, you'll need to get one—the court always demands respect, so it doesn't "please the court" (legal pun) if you show up in torn jeans and an "I'm a Belieber" t-shirt. Also, be prepared for the panel of judges to tear you and your argument apart mercilessly—I've seen many a law student who thought they were well-prepared be reduced to tears in about ten-seconds flat. "My dog could make a better argument than that," screams a judge in your face, "and my dog's dead!" After doing their best to convince you that you are little more than an illiterate wretch who lacks the mental prowess to operate a Pez dispenser, they'll then wrap things up by saying something like "but hey, great job." You'll leave feeling humiliated and confused, and the best part of it all is remembering that you paid to be treated that way.

Finally, here's the part where I warn you about how soul-crushing law school can be, especially if you're not ready for what's about to come. I'll start with grades. Grading in law school is almost always done on a strict, non-negotiable curve. Some schools offer letter grades, some schools offer something a bit different (like High Honors, Honors, Pass, Fail). If only 5% can get the grade of A, and you're in a class with 100 students, only 5 can get an A. If that fifth student has a final grade of 91.6, and you have a 91.5, you're getting a B, and there's nothing you can do about it. What that does is create an extraordinarily competitive and cut-throat environment in law school, and competitive, cut-throat environments often turn people into nasty, horrible, cruel, and vindictive human beings. What this means for you is that (1) you quickly develop the sinking suspicion that you are surrounded by the biggest collection of douche-bags ever assembled; (2) you alternatively feel that you are surrounded by effortlessly brilliant people and somehow they let you in to law school as the token idiot who provides a bit of comic relief; or (3) you wake up one day and realize you've become that person you said you'd never become.

On top of that, law school is a professional school, and part of your law school experience will be to socialize you into the legal profession. Part of that socialization will come from your fellow law students, and part of that will come from the culture of your law school. What it can do, however, is really toy with your identity and your sense of self-worth, even without you realizing it. Students who show up on day one with long hair, a scruffy beard, and an old pair of sandals, vowing they'll never sell out, often end up sporting a suit, a clean shave, and a lawyerish haircut even before they finish their first semester. This is yet another reason I almost always advise potential law school applicants to take a year or two off before law school. Part of that time can be spent figuring out who you are, what you are made of, and what you really want out of life. You'd be surprised how few people actually take the time to do that. If you show up as a 1L with your sense of self firmly in hand, or in heart, as it were, then you'll have a much better chance of leaving law school as the person you always dreamed you'd be.

CHAPTER 24

WHAT'S LAW SCHOOL LIKE?
THE SECOND YEAR (2L)

After the intensity of the first year and your summer internship, the start of your second year can feel like a breath of fresh air. Your course options open up quite a bit—maybe you'll take Native American law, or animal law, or perhaps now is the time when you decide to explore the world of international law and human rights. Plus you've got one year behind you and law school seems so familiar to you now. You found your groove, and it's all perfectly legal.

One thing you might end up doing as a 2L is joining a law review. Law reviews are student-run law journals that publish the works of law professors and legal professionals on a wide variety of topics. Many of them are quite prestigious, too, so you can feel like you are really on the cutting edge of legal scholarship during your time on law review. I do need to back up a bit on this, however, in that if you're thinking of joining a law review as a 2L, you would most likely try out for it as a 1L (as if you didn't already have enough on your plate). Trying out for law review usually consists of submitting a writing sample and then picking up a packet that will test your skills at editing a legal text, which will undoubtedly involve the one thing that you can't avoid in the world of law, namely, the beautiful and beautifully dreaded Bluebook. The Bluebook, which by the way is actually blue, is the guidebook for how to cite things properly in legal citation format. In law school, the Bluebook becomes a verb. If you're on a law review and a manuscript is handed to you, you might be told to "Bluebook it," meaning you get to check each and every reference and footnote to make sure they have all been cited properly. Oh, and by the way, law review manuscripts can run to well over 100 pages, and since the field of law is all about evidence, it's possible that nearly every sentence will have at least one reference, and quite often more than one. If you get selected for law review based on your try out as a 1L, then law review will be a new part of your life as a 2L.

As a 2L you might also opt for some more hands-on types of things. Many law schools, in fact most law schools, offer what are sometimes called "clinics." In spite of what the name suggests, there's nothing medical about them. What a legal clinic does is give you a chance to work with faculty and/or other legal professionals in an environment where you work directly on an ongoing case or project. You might even be paired with a specific client, though there are of course limits to what you can do since you are not yet at this point a lawyer. In this sense, it's more like a legal apprenticeship. There are human rights clinics, immigration clinics, refugee clinics—all sorts of possibilities. Sometimes the kinds of clinics that are offered simply depends on the specialization of the law school faculty, so if this sounds appealing to you, when you are doing your preliminary research and getting your applications together (see my earlier chapter on this if you don't know what I'm talking about), check out what legal clinics are offered at the law schools to which you want to apply.

In case you think this all sounds like a walk in the park compared to being a 1L, well, here's the part where I tell you about what will undoubtedly be the centerpiece of your life as a 2L, and, I might add, the source of your greatest anxiety. I am referring here of course to OCIs, otherwise known as On Campus Interviews. You might remember from the previous chapter that I said the internship you do during the summer after your first year is extraordinarily important as it may help define the direction in which you want your legal career to evolve. The reason it is of such importance is that during your first semester as a 2L, there will be a week known as OCI week (or some such name), and this is the week when representatives from all sorts of law firms and other legal employment venues (for example, the State Department) descend upon campus to give first-round interviews to law students. If you're thinking, "wait, what?" then I'll spell it out for you: in your third semester of law school you will go through your first round of interviews for what might end up being your first major career move as a lawyer. That's why life as a 1L is such a pressure cooker—you've got two semesters and a summer to build up a legal resume impressive enough to make law firms want to interview you.

After the intensity of OCI week, you can get back to the joy-fest of your regularly-scheduled semester, but don't think for a moment it's all just back to legal business as usual. You see, OCI week is just the *first* round of interviews, a chance for law firms and others to determine if they think you're worth the time and money for a more in-depth interview. Those interviews, the second round wine-and-dine interviews (often referred to as "fly backs") happen in the second semester of your time as a 2L. That means on top of all the other things you are doing as a 2L, you have to find a way to cope with the lingering background radiation of anxiety that sets in from the moment you finish OCI week until the moment you actually get an offer for a second round interview.

If you do get the call for a fly back interview, you'll of course have to prepare for it in due course. The good news is that whoever wants to interview you will treat you like royalty because in essence they are at this point trying to recruit you—they arrange and pay for everything, and you're job is to impress them. If they're going to make you an offer, you'll have it in hand before the end of your second semester as a 2L. That's right, it's very possible you'll already have your first job before you finish your second year of law school (if you're wondering why you need to continue for another year, that's in the next chapter). If you do get an offer—and if you get multiple offers you'll have to choose just one—you'll probably spend the summer after your second year working in some capacity for the law firm or organization that made you the offer.

And yes, it's possible that you won't get a second round interview, and if you do, it's possible you won't get an offer. This goes back to the point I made in the previous chapter about the emotional toll of law school. It can make you feel like a complete failure to watch fellow law students talking about their amazing offers and smiling like there's been a leak at the nitrous oxide factory while you have what appears to be nothing to show for all your hard work. In those moments you have to find some inner strength and keep the faith in yourself—don't let law school crush your soul and self-respect. Maybe you made some mistakes, and so this is the time to learn from them. Or maybe you didn't make any mistakes, and what you've learned from this is that the standard legal path just isn't for you. You're different, and that's cool, and now all you need to do is figure out what legal path *will* work for you. Trust me, there's a path for everyone. You just need to find the one that works for you.

CHAPTER 25

WHAT'S LAW SCHOOL LIKE?
THE THIRD YEAR (3L)

If Charles Dickens were to write something about being a 3L, he'd probably describe it as the best of times and the worst of times. It sounds like the kind of thing he'd say. At this point in your law school trajectory, there's a good chance you've already landed a job, you've already taken the essential classes, and you've already figured out for the most part in which legal direction you want to go when you leave law school at the end of your third year. That probably sounds like the best of times, so what part could possibly be the worst of times?

First let me tell you what life is like for a 3L. The classes you take as a 3L will for the most part be only things you choose to take either because they look inherently interesting or because they cover an area of law that you now recognize might be important and helpful as you prepare to launch your legal career. For the 1L crowd, the 3Ls seem a little aloof, like they've got other things on their mind, and the fact is, they do. If you were on law review as a 2L, then you might have opted to run for a spot on the ed board (editorial board), and if you were successful in your bid, you'll also be doing your duties as an ed board member as a 3L. If you joined a legal clinic as a 2L, you might continue that work as a 3L as well.

For most 3Ls, however, the big legal elephant in the law school room is the bar exam. If you secured a position at a law firm—maybe you even landed your dream job—as a 2L, it really starts to hit you as a 3L that your job offer is contingent on you passing the bar. You'll start studying for the bar exam, possibly taking classes in areas where you feel your knowledge isn't as solid as you want and possibly even taking bar exam review classes (sort of like the classes you might have taken for the LSAT). I'll talk more about the bar exam in the next chapter, but for now, just understand that as a 3L, having the bar exam waiting for you at the end of law school can make you feel like you are a runner at the start of a race that has one infinitely tall hurdle that you somehow have to jump over to get to the legal career that awaits you at the finish line.

So your time as a 3L will be the best of times because in many ways the pressure of law school is beginning to ease. You can actually enjoy your classes rather than worry about them because you need to impress a prospective employer. But it's also the worst of times because you realize that life as a 3L isn't really the end of law school but rather a transitional year in which you move from law student to legal professional and have to muster up the energy and commitment to pass the bar exam. The bar exam really is its own complex beast, so it deserves a chapter all to itself, which I'll serve up next in this ongoing buffet of delicious information.

CHAPTER 26

WHAT'S THE BAR EXAM ALL ABOUT?

Remember the feeling you had as an undergrad when you got your degree and jumped with joy because you were finally done? No more finals—woohoo! When you get your JD, you won't have that feeling. Sure, you'll be relieved that law school is over and you should certainly celebrate your accomplishment, but the tough part isn't quite over yet because now you have to pass the bar exam. There are a few exceptions to this, but the majority of law school graduates go straight from the frying pan of law school into the fire of the bar exam. I know that makes the bar exam sound a bit like hell, but if you queried a sampling of those who actually took the exam, I'm sure they'd tell you that's a fairly accurate assessment.

Earlier I mentioned that the primary purpose of law school is to prepare you for the bar exam. That's definitely true, but it's true primarily in terms of the content and the mechanics of law as a field of study. Law school is not a three-year bar exam prep class, and next to nothing is taught in law school about how to prepare for the bar exam itself or what's even going to be on it. That's why most freshly-minted JD recipients celebrate the end of law school by signing up for bar exam prep classes. Not only do they need to strategize about how to take the bar exam, but they also realize that all those essential "boot camp" classes they took as a 1L—well, that was almost three years ago, and you can forget a lot in three years. Bar exam prep means reviewing everything you learned in law school and brushing up on all of it, while at the same time learning how to best prepare a strategy for the exam itself. There's no way around it—it's a lot of work. Woohoo!

The bar exam isn't offered every week or even every month. It's offered once a year, though there are some states where it is offered twice a year. That means if you have a job waiting for you and it's contingent on passing the bar, you have an insane amount of pressure to make sure you pass it the first time. You can definitely take the bar exam again— and most jurisdictions allow you to take it as many times as you like until you pass—but having to tell an employer that you didn't pass the bar exam and won't be able to perform the job for which you were hired for another twelve months will certainly put you in the legal dog house. In other words, you need to be really well prepared for the bar exam, and you need to start preparing for it even before your last year of law school is finished.

The California bar exam scheduled for 2017, for example, took place on July 25 and 26. California used to have a three-day bar exam, but as of 2017, it now has a two-day exam with both morning and afternoon sessions. You have to register in advance so you would have done that most likely in your last semester of law school. It's also expensive to take the bar exam, so aside from the time commitment, you can be out a lot of money with nothing to show for it if you don't pass the bar. But if you look at the scheduling, keeping with our example from California, that means you would graduate in May with your JD, and then immediately go into a two-month crash-course in everything you studied in law school and also in how to best prepare for the exam. So the real celebration of law school isn't when you get your JD. It's when you pass the bar exam. And when you do pass the bar exam, you get the most wonderful reward of all. You get to go to work.

What's on the bar exam? The content varies year to year, but it draws from a pretty predictable list of legal subjects: business and corporations, civil procedure, property, contracts, criminal law, criminal procedure, rules of evidence, professional responsibility (legal ethics), torts, trusts, wills, and so forth. There will be multiple choice questions and also essay questions, and for the most part you can plan on a very grueling experience. There is a multi-state bar exam (MBE) as well as the part of the exam specific to the state where you want to practice law. Some of those state-specific exams are much more difficult than others—the California bar exam, for instance, has always been seen as one of the most difficult. California just *has* to be different.

It is possible, by the way, to take the bar exam without ever going to law school. Many states have specific regulations for this, however, so don't think you can just sign up and give it a go. Because it takes a lot of time and work to grade the bar exam (especially the essays), they don't want you wasting their time by taking the bar exam just because someone dared you to or just because you were bored to tears and thought the bar exam was just the thing to cure your ennui. Most states therefore require you to complete a sort of apprenticeship or mentorship with a practicing legal professional, who basically has to vouch for you to say that you are sufficiently ready to take the bar exam as a serious candidate. We're not talking about a summer internship. We're talking a multi-year apprenticeship (4-5 years) with a specific number of minimum hours each week. Some states require you to have at least one year of law school under your belt, too. People have certainly taken the bar exam and passed it without going to law school, and while it might be cheaper than going to law school, it isn't necessarily easier.

CHAPTER 27

DO I HAVE TO TAKE THE BAR EXAM?

Well, it depends on what you want to do. You definitely have to take the bar exam (and pass it) if you want to practice law, as in, be a lawyer in the traditional sense of the word. Once you pass the bar, you will then join the bar association (and possibly more than one), which provides the credentials that allow you to interact professionally and officially with all the relevant legal institutions in the jurisdiction where you practice law. Every jurisdiction, whether state or federal, has its own bar association so there's really no way around it.

There are, however, other areas of legal activity where taking the bar exam may not be required. If you pursue international law, for instance, then you should know that there is no international bar exam. Before you clap your hands with delight and declare that international law is definitely the path for you, you should know that even though international law has no bar exam, passing the bar exam in a domestic jurisdiction may be either a requirement or a considerable asset even if you are working for an international law firm. International law cases are frequently heard in domestic courts, and if you didn't take the bar exam and join the bar association, when the key moment comes for the case to go to court, you can't be a part of the team. As I mentioned in an earlier chapter, human rights law is considered a branch of international law, but nearly all human rights cases play out in domestic courts. If you want to be a human rights lawyer, you'll probably want to take the bar.

If you are thinking of working for an international institution such as the United Nations, or for a non-governmental organization (NGO), in a position where you use your legal knowledge but are not necessarily practicing law (not taking clients and not arguing cases), strictly speaking you would not need to take the bar exam. But even here there are other factors to consider that might incline you to take the bar exam anyway. Nearly all the jobs for which you would apply in these types of organizations are going to be fiercely competitive. Credentials can come into play in making the final decision about whom to hire, and if it comes down to you and one other person, and that other person has passed the bar and you never even took it, that may be the just the thing that gives the job to your competition. Another reason you might still want to consider taking the bar exam is that law careers usually don't just stay on one straight and narrow path. Perhaps you work for an NGO for ten years, and at that point you decide it's time for a change—a law firm makes you an offer. Do you know how much harder it will be for you to prepare for the bar exam after a ten year gap from law school? In other words, if you decide not to take the bar exam after law school, then be very, very sure about your decision.

Of course, if you are going to be practicing law in another country, then taking the bar exam in the US might not make much sense. For the same reason listed above, however, you still might consider taking the bar exam in the US anyway. It's an attractive asset to a foreign law firm to have a lawyer from the US who could, if needed, participate in proceedings in the US. Things can also change for a variety of reasons—you might get a better job offer back in the US, or you might meet the love of your life and your one true love absolutely needs you to be back in the US, or you might just have one of those moments in life where you decide you miss being in the US and want to return. But before all that happens, do keep in mind that other countries will usually have their own requirements to practice law, and you'll have to do the proper research to see what you need to do to be certified to practice law there.

Nevertheless, there are a number of law-related occupations that do not require you to take or pass the bar exam. I'll talk more about those fields in another chapter, but as a quick example you might decide you want to work as a legal consultant—someone who offers well-informed legal advice in a particular field (such as publishing), but not in the context of actually practicing law. If you know that's what you want to do, and can't imagine changing your mind somewhere down the road, then it is quite possible that you don't have to take the bar exam after all.

To put all that together, the short answer is that you don't *have* to take the bar exam, but there are many compelling reasons to do so. Think this through very thoroughly before you opt *not* to take the bar. As with everything else relating to law school, take a fair amount of time for reflection and consideration before you make your decision, so that you know no matter what you decide, you made the right choice.

CHAPTER 28

WHAT'S A DAY IN THE LIFE OF A LAWYER?

Considering how many different types of law there are, and how many different roles a legal professional can play, there isn't really a one-size-fits-all day-in-the-life of a lawyer. The only thing I can say that is truly universal about the day-in-the-life of a lawyer is that it will be a long one. Long hours are common for lawyers, for several reasons. If you're on a case that is going to trial, for example, you have to work within the confines of the court calendar. If the trial starts in two months and you've got four months of work to do, then you'll be working twelve-hour days seven days a week to make sure you're prepared. Oh, and there's no overtime in the legal world, though there are billable hours.

I mentioned in an earlier chapter that there's no reason to try to get a law-related job before you go to law school, thinking that some legal work experience will improve your chances of getting in (as I said, it won't). However, I've advised many students to seek out a law-related job if they aren't sure about law school because it gives them a chance to see what lawyers actually do. I would say at least half of the students who took that advice ultimately chose *not* to go to law school. Part of the reason for that choice is seeing first-hand the hard work and long hours that are common in the life of a lawyer. Another part of the reason is the realization that being a lawyer can just be a very stressful job, not only because of the pressure to meet a constant flow of deadlines, but also because of the pressure to win a constant flow of cases.

Most but not all types of legal work take place in a highly competitive environment, and that kind of environment can take both an emotional and physical toll on a person over time. On top of that, working long hours, often with one or no days off in a week, can put great strain on relationships and indeed, great strain on family life as well. It's a difficult and delicate balance to pull your weight as part of a legal team and also pull your weight as a romantic partner or family member. Note that I said difficult—not impossible.

If you want the grittiest truth about the legal scene, then listen up, because this is important—*there are a lot of lawyers out there who are fundamentally unhappy people and who genuinely hate their job.* So why do they keep doing it? Sometimes it's the most basic of reasons, which is money. They've got loans to pay off, along with all the other expenses of law school and the expenses of everyday life. Some of them might hate their job simply because the work environment at their particular firm or office is unbearably dreadful. They're no doubt hoping to switch to a different law firm at some point, preferably soon, but you can't just walk off and quit without incurring some serious damage to your legal career. Lawyers who are in positions they don't like also continue to stay with them because there's no guarantee that switching firms or even switching careers will put them in a better work environment. Misery is not unique to the field of law. Horrible, spiteful people can be found in pretty much any career path, and sometimes it's just the gruesome (bad) luck of the draw that you ended up working with one.

The workload of a lawyer tends to be case-driven. If you work in a law firm, you'll typically be assigned to a case by the firm, and much of your time in your first few years will be spent fighting to get one of the "juicy" or high-profile cases normally given to more experienced members of the firm. It's also possible that you will be expected to find your own cases and clients and bring them in for the benefit of the firm. If you are an in-house lawyer, meaning you work for the law division of a company or some other organization, your work might still be case-driven—perhaps the company is being sued by a rival or there has been a possible copyright infringement by another artist—but it might also consist of giving legal counsel on specific projects or simply filing for things like patents or copyrights. If you've ever wondered why lawyers can command high salaries, it is because they are expected to know the law well and not make mistakes. If your company loses a patent because you didn't file the legal paperwork properly, that's not going to endear you to your employer, and it doesn't do much for your professional reputation either. Mistakes come at a very high cost in the legal profession.

For those who aren't enamored with the idea of working for a firm, it's also possible to start your own law practice.

The good news here is that if you do that, you get to be your own boss, which means that if you end up hating your work environment, you may have some personal issues that need addressed. You also get to choose the cases you want to work on, rather than being assigned to them by someone else. The not-so-good news is that starting out can be tough, because you don't have the reputation of a well-established firm behind you, and without that, the clients you are trying to attract might be wondering whether they should trust you with their case or not. There's some financial risk involved in the beginning, too, since your income is contingent on winning cases, and those cases, as I just mentioned, can be difficult to get. It can take years to build up a private practice, but for many of those who choose that route, most would tell you that the risk has definitely been worth it in the long run.

CHAPTER 29

WHAT IF I DON'T WANT TO BE A LAWYER?

You might be wondering why anyone would go through all the time and expense of law school and then not want to be a lawyer. As it turns out, there are a surprisingly large number of people who are very interested in working in a law-related occupation but who simply do not want to be lawyers. It also turns out that are a surprisingly large number of law-related but non-lawyer occupations to choose from. Some people choose this path because they find the many obligations and duties of being a lawyer unattractive, or because being a lawyer simply isn't a part of their personality profile. Other people who choose this different path do so after spending a few years practicing as a lawyer, at which point they grow tired of it or else decide it's time to apply their legal skills and experience in a different way. It isn't necessarily an either/or choice you have to make before you graduate from law school, though it's easier to transition from lawyer to non-lawyer than the other way around, especially depending on how many years down the legal road you've traveled in your career.

One possible non-lawyer path to pursue would be government employment. Policymaking relies heavily on the law in one way or another, and it's not a coincidence that many politicians earned law degrees before turning to politics. Every branch of the US government requires legal input for a variety or reasons. The Supreme Court is the most obvious one, and while it's true you can't submit an application to be a Supreme Court justice—though it would be fun to show up and ask for one—it is also true that every Supreme Court justice has their own staff to assist them with legal research, and that is a position you *can* apply for (I'll cover that in the next chapter). The Department of Justice obviously focuses on legal matters relating to the process of governance, but so, too, do parts of the State Department and even the Armed Forces. No member of Congress wants to spend time drafting a bill without first making sure that the key elements fall within the parameters of the Constitution, so policymakers frequently seek out legal counsel when crafting their own bills or considering the bills of others. The White House of course has its own White House Counsel, who in turn depends upon the assistance of the legally-trained members of her or his staff. And don't overlook the FBI either—it is, after all, an investigative law-enforcement agency.

Much of this, though not all of it, is replicated at lower levels of government as well. State governments have analogous equivalents to the institutions of federal government, and this is where the local loyalty I talked about in an earlier chapter often comes into play. Sure, a Yale Law Degree is a mighty wonderful thing, but if a member of the Montana State Assembly is interested in drafting environmental legislation, she or he might prefer someone who grew up in Montana or studied law in Montana, someone who has developed an attachment to the state-level landscape, to help them craft eloquent and effective environmental policy for the great state of Montana. Most major cities also have their own need for folks with a legal education. I've never been to a meeting at city hall in either San Francisco or Los Angeles where there wasn't at least one person in attendance with a law degree. Keep in mind this applies mostly to what are considered major cities. If you want to work in a place like Calpine, California, for instance, which boasts a population of 205 people, the legal opportunities in local government are unlikely to be abundant.

Another possibility that for many people combines the best of both worlds would be working in the District Attorney's office (or actually being the District Attorney). This is still government work, but for obvious reasons it relies heavily on the lawyerly skills of arguing and winning cases. Many people are drawn to this work because there is constantly the opportunity of "fighting the good fight" and putting some very horrible people behind bars where they belong. It can still be every bit as stressful as being a lawyer in private practice or in a private firm, but for some, the stress is easier to process when you know you are fighting for justice for people who rarely have anyone to fight for them.

And please don't overlook the institution that gave you your degree to begin with—law school. Being a law professor can be a very rewarding career, and affords you the opportunity to educate future generations of law students. It also frees up creative time to pursue legal research in your own area of interest. Don't underestimate the power and influence of legal research. Lawyers frequently cite law review articles when writing legal briefs for their cases, for instance, and many of the most influential arguments we have about rethinking or changing law come from those whose job it is to think things through in the bigger picture, rather than in the immediate moment of a specific case. Law professors aren't merely ivory tower intellectuals, though. Many work as legal consultants or even join legal teams in certain cases, giving them one foot in the academic door and another in the practitioner door. Legal education is an important and essential part of the never-ending task of making sure that law works in the direction of obtaining justice as best it can. It's not a bad gig, either. I work in higher education, as one of those so-called professor types, and I've never had a single day where I didn't want to go to work, nor have I ever once uttered the phrase, "I hate my job." I genuinely love my job—not many people can say that.

There's also legal work to be done in any one of a large number of cause-oriented organizations outside of government in the private sector (both non-profit and for-profit). Groups like the Southern Poverty Law Center compile legal information on hate crimes and other things, whereas groups like the Sierra Club fight for environmental protection and preservation and often need legal assistance in that fight. The Nonhuman Rights Project is an outside-the-box organization that is actually doing some very cutting-edge legal work, and if that's the kind of thing you like, that or any similar organization might be just want you want. Some people work full-time for organizations like this, though you should know that especially in the non-profit sector, the salaries can be surprisingly low. That's why some people work part-time for these organizations and draw their main salary from some other legal job. Some even volunteer their time and expertise because they simply want to further the goals of that particular group or organization. Steven Wise, for instance, the founder and president of the Nonhuman Rights Project, is also a law professor, specializing in the field of—you guessed it—animal rights.

To sum it all up, there are lots of non-lawyer opportunities out there where you can apply your legal skills and knowledge in creative and constructive ways. It's actually difficult to think of any major sector of activity—anything from literature to liturgy—that doesn't involve law in some way. There's even a whole thing called Olympic Law, which is the law that relates to the Olympic Games (itself a subunit of a larger legal area called sports law). Perhaps you'll end up being a lawyer for the International Olympic Committee, and you'll commute to work on a bobsled (in the winter) or in a kayak (in the summer). The point is, somewhere out there in the legal universe, there's a job with your name on it. You may not know what it is, but you'll know it when you find it. And when you find it—and you will—it will be awesome.

CHAPTER 30

WHAT'S CLERKING ALL ABOUT?

It may very well be the case that, up until now, every time I talked about being a lawyer and having a legal career, you imagined yourself building a case to present to someone else, most likely a judge. Now that it's time to talk about clerking, it might be time for you to imagine yourself on the other side of the desk, sitting on the bench, as it were, and being the person to whom a case is presented (being on the bench in law, by the way, unlike in sports, is a good thing). A clerk isn't a judge, but a clerk is someone who works directly with a judge to offer advice and assistance in various matters of law that are involved in any particular case. A lot of things happen behind the scenes and outside the courtroom in determining how a case turns out, as in, how a case is decided. While judges are very well-informed about matters of the law, they frequently rely on other people to find relevant case law to assist with their evaluation of a case. They do this not because they don't know how to do it, but because it takes an enormous amount of work to put together something as comprehensive and influential as, say, a Supreme Court opinion, more work than one person could possibly do on their own, considering the case load. That's where law clerks come in.

When you reach the moment of deciding whether you should apply for a clerkship or not, in many ways you are back to the kind of deep decision-making that you went through in deciding whether or not to go to law school in the first place. One thing you shouldn't do is assume that getting a clerkship will improve your chances in the legal job market. It might do that, of course, but it's really the wrong reason to try for one. The most important thing a clerkship does is give you a whole new perspective on the judicial process, and a chance to really hone your skills as a legal professional in ways that can be a considerable asset regardless of what type of law you practice. So think of a clerkship in terms of what it will do for your understanding of the law, and not for what it will for your viability in the legal job market.

One thing you should definitely know about clerkships is that they are fiercely competitive. Like law schools, clerkships can be ranked in terms of status and prestige. At the top of the list, of course, would be the Supreme Court, "clerking for the Supremes," as it is known. If you land that gig straight out of law school, you are most certainly on your way to a very distinguished legal career. (Keep in mind that if you don't get that gig, you might still be on your way to a very distinguished legal career.) Federal clerkships are also at the top of the list—federal district courts, circuit courts, and other more specialized federal courts—and those clerkships, like clerking for the Supremes, carry with them as much prestige as they do responsibility. State level clerkships may not have all the prestige as federal ones, but they can still be invaluable in so many ways, especially depending on how you imagine your legal career evolving. As I said previously, local loyalty and local experience is highly valued by many people in the legal profession, and in some cases a clerkship in a more local context can carry more weight than a federal clerkship might, depending on the situation.

A clerkship is much more than just behind-the-scenes legal research to help a judge craft an opinion or verdict. As a clerk, you would also be involved in the day-to-day activities of everything that goes on in the judicial process, things that you wouldn't otherwise be involved with or privy to if you were arguing a case, rather than hearing one. Even if you never become a judge yourself, understanding how both sides of the system work and think can be a tremendous asset in how you approach all of your future work as a legal professional.

You might be thinking to yourself at this point—if a clerkship is such an amazing asset to have, why would anyone *not* work as a clerk? Well, it's a bit of a trade off. For the clerkship to have the full effect you want it to have, it should probably be in a field or in a level of law that you know you want to pursue. A clerkship in Federal Tax Court is nicely prestigious, what with it being in a federal court and all, but if you are hoping to work as a criminal defense attorney, then that clerkship is not going to be time well-spent, as it will do precious little to help you down the path of criminal law (unless your specialty is criminal tax evasion and white-collar crime). Similarly, if you know you want to practice law in Utah (or if that's where you got your offer as a 2L), taking a state-level clerkship in Kentucky isn't going to push your career any further along the path than merely going straight to Utah and starting your position as soon as you pass the bar.

Incidentally, soon-to-graduate law students aren't the only ones who apply for clerkships, and there are many judges out there who place higher value on experienced applicants with a few years of big-wave legal practice under their belts than on legal barneys bobbing idly in the law-school boneyard. Judges are busy people and what they don't want to do is lots of hand-holding for newbies who know a lot about the law but not the grit of how law actually works. Clerkships are competitive, and complexly so. But don't let any of that deter you from trying to get one, if a clerkship seems to be calling your name.

There are still trade-offs to consider when applying for a clerkship a few years into the game—if you are looking for a new direction for your law career it might be just what you need, but again, obtaining a clerkship is not always an automatic boost if it has no direct relevance to what you want to do. As with the decision to go to law school, think it through very carefully, do your research, and make a well-informed decision and once you do, never look back.

CHAPTER 31

DO I HAVE TO CHOOSE BETWEEN FIGHT-
ING FOR JUSTICE AND MAKING MONEY?

I n an earlier chapter I discussed how law school can really put pressure on your sense of self and your sense of
self-worth. I even suggested that one of the reasons to take
a gap year between undergrad and law school was to spend
some time with yourself to figure out what really matters to
you. I mention those things again here because when you
enter the world of the legal professional, it is easy to fall
prey to some serious emotional turmoil about the choices
you want to make or have to make. The good news is that, if
you are the type of person who went to law school because
you thought you would spend your life fighting for justice,
there are a lot of options at your disposal to help you stay
true to your vision.

I should also clarify at this point one of the great mis-
nomers about the legal profession, which is the persistent
belief that fighting for justice is the exclusive domain of
those who eschew money. The fact is that all lawyers fight

for justice—that's actually the definition of what a lawyer is—they just do so in different ways. It's easy to dismiss a corporate lawyer with a very lucrative position as a "sell out," but corporations are as entitled to fairness in the judicial process as any other actor, and they pay very well for the best legal talent they can acquire. Corporate lawyers are fighting for justice for the companies they represent. You might not like corporate lawyers, and you might one day be fighting against them, and hooray for that, but corporations are entitled to legal representation and corporate lawyers are as integral a part of the judicial process as are the lawyers who fight against them.

In a different sense, however, fighting for justice means representing those who, like corporations, are equally entitled to fairness in the judicial process but, unlike corporations, cannot pay for the type of legal assistance they need. If your idea of justice is to be the lawyer who wants to help such people, then it's a matter of simple finances that you will not be making the money a corporate lawyer will make. The real question is: are you okay with that?

During your time as a law student, you will discover very quickly that there is a persistent orthodoxy in the legal profession that success and money are directly correlated. Successful lawyers make a lot of money, unsuccessful lawyers don't. It takes a strong sense of personal ethics not to get caught up in that mindset. The judicial system is only fair to the extent that everyone—regardless of status, power, and wealth—has equal access to the process of justice. To keep it fair, therefore, someone has to be the person who walks away from the money and toward the people who have been wronged but can't find anyone to help them or any way to pay for the help they need. Without lawyers who take the route less-traveled, the system can easily decay into injustice.

You might very well be the person who decides to take that route, and yet somewhere in the back of your mind, you know you've got a huge amount of debt to pay back, and you look at your monthly salary and then at your monthly student loan payment and quickly realize you will be making a negative salary. Living on a negative salary is tough, to say the least. So, what do you do?

One option is to look into debt forgiveness programs. There are a lot of law schools and lot of state and federal government departments and other private institutions that have a vested interest in keeping the legal system fair. To encourage people to follow professional legal paths that aren't entirely driven by salary, they offer incentives such as debt forgiveness. These incentives don't apply to every legal pathway, and there are conditions on the kind of work that they cover, but just know that there are options to pursue that will take you beyond the simple calculus of salary versus debt.

Then there is the fact that sometimes life is just an unpredictable mess. The legal system might be all about fairness and justice, but life and the legal system share little in common on this point. Maybe you have parents with health issues who will need your help, so you realize you'll have to buy a house big enough so they can live with you. Maybe you want to get married and have kids—that's a whole different type of financial consideration than living on your own and not caring that your 1993 Volvo doesn't have a backseat but does have a colorful bungee cord to keep the trunk closed.

Maybe you realize that you've struggled your whole life and the idea of a steady job with a good paycheck and good medical insurance is something you need at this point in your life. All of those things, and many other things, are possible and even likely to happen in your life, and when they do, they put you in the unenviable position where the image of yourself as the person fighting for justice and the image of yourself as the person enjoying the nice house and even nicer wine cellar start to battle each other like two comic-book rivals in an epic struggle to control the legal universe.

If you can handle some long-term, strategic planning, you can still make this work so that you don't feel like you've compromised or "sold out" on your values. One thing to know is that most law firms allow and sometimes even encourage what is known as "pro bono" work. Pro bono is work you take on without being paid—it's a Latin phrase that means "for the (common) good." Supporting pro bono work is good for the firm in terms of their public relations profile and since it also shows a commitment to keeping the system fair, it's an asset for a firm's reputation. You can seek out law firms that promote pro bono work and when you are in a position to take on a pro bono case, choose the cases where you feel that you are fighting for the kind of justice you always thought you'd fight for. The firm wins because they get good press and potentially new clients, and you win because you feel you didn't abandon your original ideals. You also win because you continue to get a salary from your law firm, which is why you take on the pro bono work in the first place.

Some people are very happy with a situation like that, and make a career of it. Others do it only as long as necessary—to pay off student loans, for example—and then leave the law firm world to pursue the path they originally wanted to pursue. The short answer is that, with a little planning and perseverance, if you don't want to make the choice between earning money and fighting for justice, you don't have to.

On a final note, don't feel guilty about wanting a good life for yourself. The people you want to represent, the ones who can't otherwise afford to navigate the legal system, what is it they are looking for? They are looking to restore a good life taken from them or to make the one they have even better, in a situation where the life they wanted or had was thwarted by a harm that desperately needs a legal remedy. The law protects the ability of people to have or pursue a good life, so there's no reason to feel guilty if you want the same for yourself. You should also understand that not everyone has the same idea of what a "good life" is, so maybe you should give some thought to that as well, to figure out what matters most to you. For some people, having a good life really does mean having a lot of money. For others, it means having a lot of time to spend with family and friends. In the best of possible worlds, the legal path you want to follow and the good life you want to lead will move in tandem, side-by-side and step-by-step. That's not an impossible dream. With a little work, you really can make it happen.

CHAPTER 32

THOSE LAWYER JOKES—ARE LAWYERS REALLY BAD PEOPLE?

How do you know when a lawyer is lying?
His lips are moving.

Clever, eh? There's a ton of lawyer jokes out there and nearly all of them are both hilariously funny and uncomfortably mean—seems a lot of people really hate lawyers. Lawyers have heard these jokes, too, and in case you are wondering, they do tell them to each other and have a good laugh over them. It might surprise you to hear, however, that the vast majority of lawyers in the US are passionately ethical about their craft. Sure, there are bad lawyers—all it takes is a few bad legal eggs to sully the integrity of the profession. But there are also bad doctors, and bad farmers, and bad teachers, and bad actors, and yet when was the last time you heard of a whole genre of, say, teacher jokes? There is something particularly pernicious about how lawyer jokes portray those who practice law, and

I think the vindictiveness of those jokes stems less from the alleged immoral and greedy nature of lawyers than it does from the sense of powerlessness that comes from needing someone else to argue on one's own behalf. We don't like feeling powerless, and lawyer jokes empower us by making us feel like we're settling a score that, quite frankly, doesn't need to be settled.

If you've ever known someone who is a lawyer and asked them for legal advice, you might have been surprised by their rather dodgy or non-committal reaction. Or they might have suddenly given a professional disclaimer that seems to come out of nowhere: "I want to make clear this is not professional legal counsel..." or something like that. From your perspective, you might have suddenly thought this person—let's make her a friend of yours—to be just one more douchebag lawyer who thinks she's smarter than you. But the reality is that legal ethics is involved even in the most informal legal question or request for legal advice, and when you ask a lawyer for this type of information, you can put them in an awkward situation. On the one hand, they want to be a good friend or friendly acquaintance, but on the other, they have to stay true to the requirements of legal ethics. If the advice they give you is any way a professional act, it becomes something of a contract, which means for instance that you can hold the lawyer legally accountable if you follow the advice and it doesn't go well for you. You might be thinking you're not the kind of person who would sue a friend, and maybe that's true, but there are plenty of other people out there who would happily do so, and your lawyer friend cannot ethically make exceptions just because you might be a nicer person than they are.

There are in fact a plethora of ethical obligations in the legal profession, ranging from attorney-client privilege (your lawyer cannot divulge information about your case to anyone else) to the separation of professional and private communication and separation of professional and private financial transactions. Aside from the most general legal advice—"No, Matías, dry-cleaning *isn't* a foolproof way to launder money"— it's a very tricky thing for a lawyer to mix friendship with legal practice, unless you want to take the formal step of hiring your friend or paying for her legal advice.

Bar associations also take legal ethics very seriously, and clients and fellow lawyers can report derelict lawyers for breach of ethical standards to the bar association. Lawyers aren't likely to cover for each other because it then becomes a form of corruption, and can result in the tarnishing of an entire firm's reputation. Lawyers don't like to see their profession besmirched or maligned, which is why the vast majority of lawyers take the ethics of legal practice very, very seriously.

Having said that, as with any profession, there are people who make it through law school, pass the bar, and become lawyers who still manage to commit egregiously unethical acts of legal dysfunction. Forging a judge's signature to get a wiretap on a spouse's phone to gather evidence they're cheating on you, or altering documents to be presented as evidence, are both things that can get a legal professional disbarred (as in, thrown out of the bar association), but that hasn't stopped lawyers from actually doing them. The good news is that lawyers who are dumb enough to try things like that are also dumb enough to get caught, so the problem usually works its way out of the system quite naturally.

Law is a noble profession, and when done well, can lead to powerful acts of justice and transformative acts of change. Yes, there are bad lawyers, and yes, there are unethical lawyers, and yes, there are lawyers who are insufferably arrogant human beings. Those are the ones that make for great characters in movies, but most lawyers aren't in movies because for the most part, they're decent, ethical folks. So let people tell all the lawyer jokes they want. Just remember that those people, if they tell a joke about someone else that crosses a line and that someone else tries to sue them for slander, who do you think they're gonna call? I'll give you a hint: it ain't Ghostbusters.

CHAPTER 33

WHAT DOES THE (LEGAL) FUTURE HOLD?

There are actually two ways to answer this question. One is to look at what the future holds for *you*. The other is to look at what the future holds for the *law*. I'll answer both of those questions, with the added organic cherry of information atop the ice cream sundae of law that the two questions are actually more intertwined than might first appear to be the case. Talk about just desserts.

While there is the occasional legal professional who lands an amazing job right out of law school and builds their entire legal career within the same institutional setting (such as a law firm), that's more of the exception than the rule. Most lawyers switch firms or switch roles as they build their legal career, either to build a stronger and more formidable professional portfolio or because they've reached a professional plateau in one place and realize they need to go elsewhere to keep climbing higher. Also, life priorities change. Perhaps you've landed your dream job in a law firm, and you thrive on the intense and competitive work environment, to the point where working long hours seven days a week seems like an exciting lifestyle...until you meet the love of your life. Suddenly you rediscover what weekends and evenings are for, and while your new love is thrilled with your commitment and devotion, your law firm, well, not so much. You might want to find a new legal position that's slightly less adrenaline-filled and more amicable to the idea of building a relationship or starting a family.

It's also possible that the job you land out of law school might not be your dream job at all. It might even be a nightmare. If that's the case, don't fret—strategize instead. The good news is that you have a job, which means you can eat and pay bills. But you'll still want to focus on doing a good job at what you do, whether you're thrilled with it or not, because you'll need to build a good track record so you can obtain another position in a year or two that takes you one step closer to where you want to be. Opportunities will open, so always be vigilant and proactive in looking for new professional pathways to pursue. You're only stuck in a dead-end, insufferable legal career if you let yourself get stuck there.

If you are the kind of person who likes to be on the cutting edge of things, you might want to step back and ponder the future of law itself. Law is inherently a conservative, slow-moving field, building on past precedents and shying away from making rapid, radical shifts in perspective. That's great for law's ability to create a solid foundation for politics and society—there's a reason the rule of law is such a vaunted thing—but it's less than ideal for fields where rapid or uncertain change is the norm. One key area where the law struggles to keep up with things is high-tech innovation and information technology. Self-driving cars are on their way to becoming a common tech staple of our lives, but accidents are going to happen in the development of this technology that will create challenges for how to assess legal responsibility and assign blame. All forms of autonomous technology, especially as they increase in so-phistication and complexity, will create challenges for the law, especially since technology likes to evolve rapidly and the law does not.

Another field where cutting edge legal questions will emerge is in the area of biotechnology and medical re-search. Questions of self-ownership—our ability to control access to and lay legal claim to our own biological mate-rial (such as DNA)—are becoming increasingly difficult to answer. The development of new medicines and access to those medicines raises questions of fairness and life priori-tization, many of which have an essential legal component to them.

Even in what seems like the more straightforward areas of legal activity, it has become clear that law plays a sur-prisingly powerful role in tempering things like political volatility. The intense rush of political action that was set in motion with the start of a new presidency in January 2017, for instance, was almost immediately rerouted from politi-cal institutions to legal ones. Legal experts from both sides of the political spectrum suddenly found themselves to be key actors in trying to find legal solutions to political chal-lenges. Whether it was the White House trying to argue its case for a travel ban, or the American Civil Liberties Union trying to argue its case against it, the power that law holds in ensuring the stability and viability of democracy has turned out to be both formidable and indispensable.

The main point here is that law is a dynamic field, so it should come as no surprise that a legal career can be quite dynamic as well. The legal path you choose to follow as you go forth into the future can be one full of cutting-edge uncertainty or it can be full of precedent-based stability. Which of those paths you follow depends more on you than you might think—there's no need to surrender your personal autonomy at any point in your legal career. Law might be an inherently conservative force, in that it tends to favor stable increments of change, but neither the force of law nor the change it creates can thrive on complacency. The same therefore holds true for those who safeguard the integrity of the law. Legal professionals can't afford to be complacent—ever—which is yet another reason why law can be such an exciting and dynamic professional craft to practice. The future is unwritten, but when it finally comes to pass, one thing that is absolutely certain is that when we find the words to describe it, many of those words will be drawn from and inspired by the language of the law. And who knows—maybe you'll be the one to write them.

CHAPTER 34

CAN YOU TELL ME AN INSPIRING STORY ABOUT LAW?

S ure can. In fact, I could tell you several inspiring stories about law, but I'll just stick with one for now. I'd like to tell you a very brief story of one of my legal heroes (life hero, too), B. R. Ambedkar (as in Bhimrao Ramji Ambedkar). My choice might seem a little unorthodox, unless you happen to be from India, but there is a connection to the US involved, and in any case, it's always good to broaden your horizons to understand how the law can play such a transformative role in pretty much every country and culture around the world. So grab yourself a nice *chole bhature*, or *dahi pakora*, or live on the edge and go for the *pesarattu*, and read on for your daily dose—or should I say daily *dosa?*—of legal inspiration.

B. R. Ambedkar was born in Central India, in what is now the state of Madhya Pradesh, in 1891. While I don't have time here to go into the intricate complexities of what is known as the caste system in India, the main point to understand here is that Ambedkar was from a caste group that were considered to be at the absolute bottom of the caste hierarchy, a group known today as the Dalits (Dalits is a collective category and comprises a vast array of different groups, all with equally low status). Ambedkar thus faced severe discrimination right from birth. In school, for instance, he had to sit separately from all the other students, and was not allowed to drink water unless someone of higher status poured it into a separate cup that only Ambedkar could touch. Ambedkar thus grew up experiencing first-hand a brutal environment of persistent injustice and discrimination, something that deeply and directly influenced nearly everything he did for the rest of his life.

In spite of the discrimination he faced growing up, Ambedkar was a keen and brilliant student. He eventually received a scholarship to continue his higher education, and, after completing a degree in economics and political science at the University of Bombay, in 1913 he came to the United States to pursue his graduate studies at Columbia University. He earned an M.A. and PhD in economics from Columbia, but even with that impressive set of accomplishments, Ambedkar was not yet done. From Columbia, he went to the London School of Economics (LSE), where he earned a second PhD (an Sc.D. in the LSE system) in economics, and quite impressively did so while he was studying for the Bar in the UK legal system. He was admitted to the Bar at Gray's Inn in 1923 (going back to my earlier chapter on comparative law, remember that legal studies in the UK are quite different from the American system).

All of that would certainly suffice to consider Ambedkar an inspiring figure. Such a passion for and commitment to the opportunities afforded by higher education are rarely found among students, whether in Ambedkar's time or in our own. But that's not the most impressive part of the story. What truly impresses and indeed inspires is that Ambedkar utilized his knowledge of the law to fight injustice everywhere he found it in India, and eventually went on to become not just the first Minister of Law in India after independence in August 1947, but also the chief architect of India's constitution. Ambedkar deeply believed that the law could create justice and create a better life for all. India's constitution, which remains the longest constitution in the world, is a solid and eloquent document, one that, unlike the case in so many other newly-independent states, has stood the test of time and remains the foundation for the entire apparatus of government and law in present-day India.

Ambedkar was in many ways a human rights pioneer, even before human rights were a thing in international law and politics. He didn't just want to use law to abolish the practice of untouchability in India, he also advocated for equal rights for women, as well as for economically marginalized communities. He may have had his many political battles in trying to push his vision of justice forward—and indeed, many of those battles he lost—but he never stopped fighting and he never stopped believing that well-written laws had the power to transform not just a country but also all of humanity into a better society where justice was equally available *to* all and justice was equally provided *for* all. I know that everyone knows the name Gandhi (who by the way also originally studied to become a lawyer), but if nothing else, I hope this little story gets more people outside of

India to know the name Ambedkar, and also provides a bit of inspiration to drive your knowledge of the law in the best direction it can go.

CHAPTER 35

CAN YOU RECOMMEND THINGS ABOUT LAW FOR ME TO READ, SEE, AND HEAR?

Now that you've come this far and know everything you need to know about law school in a most epic and awesome way, it's time to reward yourself with the sort of guilty legal pleasure that only entertainment can provide. Yes, I know, in an earlier chapter I made the claim that you need to mentally jettison everything you gleaned about lawyers and the law from Hollywood movies and other forms of entertainment, but that was then and this is now. It's time to break loose a bit. To help with that, I've got all sorts of recommendations that relate in some way to law or justice, so it means you get to read, see, and hear some great stuff and still feel like you're never straying too far from what at this point just might just be your chosen career path. Mind you, there should also be days when you will want to wander very, very far away from your chosen career path, because wandering is always a good thing, but for the days when you feel like you're in the mood for a legal groove, here are some recommendations to get you started.

I should point out that in making my recommendations, I've tried to think of selections that don't usually show up on standard top ten lists, since most of those works are pretty predictable and have already been recommended countless times on countless other must-read lists. So if you're looking for Harper Lee's *To Kill a Mockingbird*, which admittedly is a great legal read, or pretty much anything written by John Grisham, whose books are deservedly held in high regard, you won't find any of that kind of stuff here. My goal here is to recommend things you *won't* find elsewhere, just so you can have the coolest and most exquisite reading, viewing, and listening lists ever legally assembled in legal history.

═══╬ ╬═══

Books

First, we'll start with books, and here I'm going to stick with fiction. The "legal thriller" is of course a whole genre unto itself, and many authors excel in this field of literary endeavor. Truman Capote's *In Cold Blood* remains a classic in this genre, and deservedly so. Many other books would be obvious choices for a must-read list of recommended legal readings, such as Jonathan Harr's *A Civil Action*, and their compelling narratives certainly hold up well under scrutiny and in many ways they live up to the hype that surrounds them. There are also books you might have already read or heard about at one point in your life and never thought of them as works of legal fiction, yet they can be read (or re-read) as such and with great reward, I should add. In this category I might include works such as Franz Kafka's *The Trial*, Herman Melville's *Billy Budd*, Arthur Miller's *The Crucible*, or Charles Dickens' *Bleak House*.

I should also make special mention here of Fyodor Dostoevsky's novel *Crime and Punishment* (1866), because even though it would be a fairly obvious choice for any reading list on law and criminality, it does do one thing better than perhaps any other work of fiction and does so in a way that still bedazzles any reader who enters its prosaic world, even a century and a half after its initial publication. In the field of criminal law, you see, there is a thing called *mens rea*. *Mens rea* is a Latin term that is usually translated as "guilty mind," and refers to the mental state of an individual who has committed a criminal act. Legal culpability for a criminal act generally requires the perpetrator to have a guilty mind or conscience, that is, to be aware of the wrongness of the act at the time the act was committed. Dostoevsky's depiction of Raskolnikov's *mens rea* (Raskolnikov is the protagonist), after he has murdered a woman in her apartment, is perhaps the finest literary description of the mental consequences of a criminal act, and of the ways that guilt becomes its own sort of punishment, aside from whatever the law might impose. Dostoevsky's classic novel remains an endlessly-engaging legal read, and is well worth the time to savor its brilliance.

As I said, however, my recommendations will (hopefully) be suggestions that you won't find on other, more standard, top ten-style lists for books about law, justice, and criminality. My recommendations aren't ranked, either, as I think all of them are equally worth exploring. So please, put on your explorer's outfit—which for a good book need only be cozy pajamas, or even just a well-worn T-shirt—and get busy exploring.

Ryunosuke Akutagawa, *Rashomon* (1915)

This novella by Japanese author Ryunosuke Akutagawa offers extraordinary insight into the way people justify their wrongful actions and how crime and guilt are far more fluid and indeterminate things than we often imagine. The story details an encounter between a man and a woman, both of whom are in desperate circumstances. The man faces almost certain death by starvation if he doesn't steal from others in order to obtain food, yet when he comes across the woman robbing a corpse, he is so outraged and disgusted that he vows never to become a thief, even if it means starvation. The woman responds by explaining that the corpse she is robbing was actually that of a woman who cheated others during her life, so robbing her to survive is not really a crime. It's an amazing short work that delves deeply into the psychological layers of crime, punishment, and guilt.

Michael Ondaatje, *Anil's Ghost* (2000)

Most people know Michael Ondaatje for his novel *The English Patient*, which was eventually made into a movie that was beloved by many but certainly not by Elaine Benes. *Anil's Ghost* is a very different sort of novel than *The English Patient*, and to my mind represents one of the finest literary expressions of what might be termed human rights literature. Anil is sent to Sri Lanka to investigate claims of human rights violations and war crimes, and she is entrusted by the UN with the task of forensically reconstructing the identity of a skeleton that bears the hallmarks of an unnatural, violent death. Anil is originally from Sri Lanka, and so faces various pressures not to pursue the investigation as thoroughly as she knows she must. No other work of fiction captures so definitively the difficult task of negotiating personal and national identity in the pursuit of justice, in this case in the context of Sri Lanka's excruciatingly brutal civil war (1983-2009).

Shakespeare, *The Merchant of Venice* (1596-98)
Shakespeare never fails to disappoint. This particular play has as its centerpiece the legal resolution of a dispute over a loan between Shylock, a moneylender, and Bassanio, a Venetian nobleman who takes the loan in order to pursue the beautiful Portia and win her heart. When the loan cannot be repaid and Shylock famously demands his pound of flesh from Bassanio, Portia steps in to the legal proceedings disguised as a (male) doctor of the law and offers an eloquent and clever argument to save the day. Yes, there is some controversy surrounding this play, largely for its depiction of Shylock (as a Jewish moneylender), but I'm putting it on the list here because of its intriguing legal content, and because it's by Shakespeare, who is simply amazing.

Halldór Laxness, *Iceland's Bell* (1943-46)
Halldór Laxness was an author of almost unsettlingly creative powers. He single-handedly modernized and redefined the saga tradition of Icelandic literature, and in doing so, still managed to spin a staggering number of new

and different worlds with each of his books. *Iceland's Bell* is no exception. This is a novel that offers an unflinchingly stark depiction of the struggle to survive in eighteenth-century Iceland, at a time when Iceland was under the yoke of Danish colonial rulers (that's right, colonialism took place within Europe, too). At the heart of this story is the tale of Jon Hreggvidsson, who is the target of legal action by colonial authorities for insulting Denmark's king and who has additionally been falsely accused of murder. In his efforts to clear his name and prove his innocence, he is defended by Snaefridur Eydalin, a headstrong and fiercely principled woman who represents not just defiance and justice but also Iceland's growing desire for independence. This is a novel worth reading not just for the depiction of law and justice in eighteenth-century Iceland, but also for the way that, through the character of Snaefridur, Laxness gives us a massively solid icon of the presence and power of women in law.

Chinua Achebe, *Things Fall Apart* (1958)

There are many reasons to read Chinua Achebe's novel *Things Fall Apart*, and there are many ways to read it as well. It's the kind of novel that means something different every time you read it. It is most often read as a tragic depiction of the cultural destruction brought by European colonialism in Africa, but I am going to recommend it for a different reason. From a legal standpoint, Achebe's novel, set as it is in Nigeria, does a masterful job of portraying different cultural ideas of law and justice, many of which may strike the reader not only as profoundly different but also as profoundly unjust. Achebe masterfully draws a parallel between the tensions and conflicts that arise between two local villages and the ways these tensions and conflicts are resolved, and the separate tensions and conflicts that arise between all of local society and the arrival of white colonial officials and missionaries. I won't give away the ending, but the story concludes with a very different type of courtroom drama, one where the two systems of justice, local and colonial, come together to create a tragic portent of things to come.

José Rizal, *Noli Me Tangere* (1887)

It's lugubriously lamentable that not more people know about the works of José Rizal. Unless you are from the Philippines, or are of Filipino heritage, or have some other reason to be connected to the Philippines, chances are you've never heard of José Rizal. I wouldn't recommend reading even a short biography of Rizal while you are writing your personal statement for law school, because learning about the things this unbelievably talented and creative Filipino polymath accomplished in his life before he was tragically executed by Spanish colonial authorities at the very young age of 35 would make anyone feel like they've been little more than lazy, indolent, and inadequate in life.

This novel by José Rizal, along with its follow-up *El Filibusterismo*, is a genuine masterpiece of world literature. Originally written in Spanish, it is widely available in English translation. *Noli Me Tangere* is not a book that focuses on the law itself, but rather one that focuses on the pervasive sense of injustice in the Philippines, during the period of Spanish colonial rule, with the implicit argument that injustice festers where the law is corrupt or weak. It is also an interesting read for Rizal's detailed insights into canon law (the laws of the Catholic Church), and how the messy overlap between the institutions of the church and the institutions of the state creates a muddled jurisdiction that collectively weakens the ability of both church and state to provide justice to the people they supposedly serve.

Ghassan Kanafani, *Men in the Sun* (1962)
There's a ton of controversy associated with anything involving Israel and Palestine, and there's even more of it when Ghassan Kanafani is involved, as he was not just a Palestinian author but also a political activist, one who was assassinated in Beirut in 1972 (at the age of 36) by what turned out to be Mossad agents. I'm not recommending this novella of Ghassan Kanafani because of some political statement I want to make. Quite the opposite, in fact—so please don't let politics and controversy get in the way here. I'm recommending it for the literary and legal statement it makes. There are few literary works that more powerfully and painfully depict the suffering and trauma of refugees than this novella by Ghassan Kanafani. In this novella, the drama involves three Palestinian refugees trying to travel from Iraq, where they are prevented from working, to Kuwait, where they could find work but first have to enter the country illegally. They pay a lorry driver to smuggle them into Kuwait, and the result is a heart-breaking statement on the suffering of refugees all around the world, Palestinian or otherwise. At a time when the word "refugee crisis" appears in headlines on a daily basis, Ghassan

Kanafani's work stands as an eloquent emotional reminder of the individual humanity that exists in the story of every refugee.

━━╪╶ ╶╪━━

Films

Next we'll move on to movies, with the same caveats as before—namely, that I'm recommending films that don't normally show up on standard must-see lists of movies about the law. There are lots of great movies out there that use law as the central device for generating dramatic tension. Classic films like *12 Angry Men* (1957) or Hitchcock's *Strangers on a Train* (1951) deal directly or indirectly with central elements of the law, the former focusing on how a jury that may or may not be made of peers agonizes over a decision, the latter focusing on how two people aim to confound and elude the entire criminal justice system by plotting two murders without motive. A more recent classic like *A Few Good Men* (1992) offers courtroom drama with a slight twist, in this case the twist being that military law is involved, whereas *The People vs. Larry Flynt* (1996) uses a real First Amendment case as its centerpiece and lets the drama of the law itself do the talking.

Special mention should also be made here of one of the greatest movies ever made in any country and in any era, and here of course I am talking about the film *Point Break* (1991)—*not* the inexecrable 2015 remake, which is vomitously awful and may possibly constitute a crime against humanity, but the 1991 original, featuring the agile Keanu Reeves, the graceful Patrick Swayze, and the always eloquent Gary

Busey. There are many reasons to recommend *Point Break*, but perhaps the most relevant one for our purposes here is for the way it offers the dramatic portrayal of a person who goes to law school and then becomes an F...B...I...Agent! (Note: only cool people will get that reference.)

I'm also not going to separate these films by genre, so drama and documentary commingle in the following list of recommendations. Will that be a problem for you? Deal with it.

The Act of Killing (2012-2013)

There are few if any documentaries like *The Act of Killing*. This is an expressively creative documentary about the traumatic events that brought Indonesia to its knees in 1965-66. The year that marked the tumultuous transitional period that occurred with the ousting of one leader (Sukarno) and the installation of another (Suharto), sometimes referred to as the "year of living dangerously" (itself depicted quite brilliantly in the eponymous dramatic film by Peter Weir), involved the mass killing of suspected communists throughout the island nation in increasingly aggressive and vicious ways. This was both witch-hunt and blood-bath. It was a time so violent and traumatic that to this day many people in Indonesia simply do not want to talk about or remember it. This is what makes *The Act of Killing* such an important film, as it puts these events front and center. Director Joshua Oppenheimer is interested in the profound question of how any human being could carry out such despicable and violent acts, and he focuses on the culpability of one Anwar Congo, who agrees to re-enact the killings in dramatic and often bizarre ways. Rarely do we get to see a person's guilty conscience come to the surface as it does in this film, making it one of the most unsettling films about the creation of *mens rea* (mentioned earlier in discussing Dostoevsky) ever made.

India's Daughter (2015)

Before I tell you what this movie is about, I am going to give you a warning: this may be one of the most difficult and disturbing films you'll ever watch. I'm not joking or exaggerating, so please take that warning seriously.

India's Daughter is a documentary by Leslee Udwin that focuses on the indescribably brutal rape and murder of Jyoti Singh in Delhi in 2012. The sheer horror of the crime sent India into a long period of painful introspection and opened a national dialogue about what has now become known as India's "rape crisis." Gender-based violence has long been a problem in India, but the enormity of the gang-rape of Jyoti Singh created a moment in which an ongoing social silence was transformed into a collective scream of pain and agony. New sensibilities about law, justice, and gender brought about by India's ever-evolving democratic modernity, clash disturbingly with deeply-entrenched cultural biases towards women that are justified in the name of tradition. Listening to the description of what happened to Jyoti Singh on that tragic night in Delhi is difficult enough, but then to listen to the perpetrators argue that they should not be in jail, let alone charged with rape, because Jyoti Singh got what she deserved, strains our ability even to utter the word humanity, let alone believe it exists.

Pink (2016)
It might seem a little unbalanced to have two films from India on a relatively short list, but there are two reasons to include *Pink* on this list. The first is that after watching *India's Daughter*, or, even if you didn't watch it but just know of the events on which it is based, you will need to watch something that might help restore your lost faith in humanity, and perhaps even inspire you to rejoin the pursuit of justice. The second reason is that *Pink* is just such an amazing gem of a film that I could not in good conscience leave it off this list. Plus it stars Amitabh Bachchan, who is one of the great cinematic treasures not just of India, but of the world.

Pink is a quintessential courtroom drama that centers around an encounter that occurred one night involving a group of young men and women, with each side telling a different version of events and with the legal system showing a clear bias against anything the women have to say. The women, it is suggested, are clearly guilty by gender. Enter one Amitabh Bachchan as a former attorney who decides to take up the case of the women, and the rest of the film is legal drama at its finest. For those coming from a background in American law and American legal drama, it's also a deeply interesting display of legal developments within a very different system of law.

Rashomon (1951)
You might think I've either made a mistake or else am being absent-mindedly redundant in recommending this film, simply because a fictional work of the same name was already on my list of must-reads. But aside from sharing the

same title, there is little to connect Ryunosuke Akutagawa's novella with Akira Kurosawa's film of the same name, though interestingly and confusingly Kurosawa's film does draw heavily from a different short-story by Akutagawa for this film. If you've never seen a film by Akira Kurosawa before, then your life is incomplete anyway, and here's your chance to make things whole again and watch one of the greatest legal films ever made.

It is often said, even in law school and among those who practice law as a profession, that law is not about the truth—it's about who can tell the most convincing story (or, in more cynical versions, the most convincing lie). This might make it seems like law is nothing more than a good story, and that justice itself is little more than an illusion, but there's more to this claim than might first appear. What *Rashomon* so brilliantly shows is that we often have no way of knowing what really happened when a crime has been committed, even when we have credible eye-witnesses to the crime itself, which means we should be able to hear the story truthfully and clearly told. It turns out that eye-witnesses rarely tell the same story about what they have seen. The film depicts four separate narratives about the same event, namely what happened to a murdered samurai whose body was found in the woods. What *Rashomon* shows is that the project of law is not to determine which of the four stories is true, but rather to accept that all four stories are true in their own way, and justice depends on creating the most convincing master-narrative we can as a legally-credible composite drawn from each of the four stories. That is the closest we will ever get to the truth.

Django Unchained (2012)
Quentin Tarantino's film *Django Unchained* is known mostly as a film about justice and redemption, but it bears remembering that at the heart of the story there is also a bit of legal detail about the practice of bounty-hunting. The narrative bit about bounty-hunting might seem an insignificant element compared to the larger injustice of slavery, but if you're going to watch *Django Unchained* as a legal drama, it becomes a central aspect of the film. Not only does bounty-hunting provide legal cover for the character of Django, as he joins forces with Dr. King Schultz tracking down wanted criminals, but it also sets up larger questions of law and justice in the midst of a system that is so profoundly unjust it offends the conscience and provokes outrage from all but the dead of heart. The film also reminds us of another easily-forgotten fact of the period: slavery was legal at the time, but not always and not everywhere. This in turn raises other troubling legal questions, such as how people in the same country could look at the same detestable practice, and yet some considered it acceptable and legal while others found it abhorrent and illegal. Difficult issues of law and order, justice and injustice, abound in this film, and those issues remain as important for our time as they were in the days in which this film is set.

On a brief side-note, there is another film I would recommend, made earlier than *Django Unchained* but set in a later time period, that raises similarly challenging questions about how egregiously exploitative and discriminatory forms of structural injustice can persist in the face of humanity. The film is called *Cry Freedom* (1987), and it documents the heart-wrenching but inspiring story of anti-apartheid activist Steve Biko (apartheid, like slavery in the antebellum South, was legal at the time it was in force, yet it was also, again like slavery, inherently unjust—one wonders how law and justice could veer so far apart from one another). I should also add that I am aware of the criticism levied at both of these films (*Django Unchained* and *Cry Freedom*) to the effect of indulging what is often called the "white savior" complex, in which a white character is considered necessary for a black character to attain their goal. I'm not going to comment on that here, as it pertains more to the style of narrative and presentation, rather than to the fundamental questions of law and injustice that each film raises. It is for the latter that I am recommending them here.

Dogani [Silenced, or also, The Crucible] (2011)
When Korean cinema came into its own as world-class cinema around two decades ago, it did so mostly on the back of blockbuster-style action movies or tear-inducing, over-the-top dramas (there were also several graphic horror films that helped pioneer the genre of "Asian horror"). Korean cinema tended to shy away from genuinely controversial issues, especially ones that involved domestic problems within South Korea, but over time exceptions began to emerge. *Dogani* is a brilliant example of one of those exceptions. The events depicted in this film are based on the true story of what happened at the Gwangju Inhwa School, a school for hearing-impaired students, in the early 2000s. Students at the school were repeatedly subjected to sexual abuse and exploitation by the faculty. When an investigation began to unearth more and more incriminating

evidence, the faculty responded by mobilizing every legal trick possible—and this movie also shows just how many legal tricks there are in the Korean legal system—to thwart the investigation or evade prosecution. The film brings up layers of legal questions relating to children's rights and the rights of disabled persons, made all the more poignant in a society where social norms make difference and disability sources of discomfort and embarrassment and where an exterior of harmony and propriety hides an ugly interior riddled with enmity and corruption. There aren't many films in the world that can claim they created new laws in their wake, but such was the pain and outrage that this film caused that the South Korean National Assembly was pressured to act and pass new protective legislation to ensure that nothing like this would ever happen again.

Ai Weiwei, *Human Flow* (2017)

Ai Weiwei is many things to many people—brilliantly-creative artist, fiercely-defiant political activist, endlessly-compassionate humanitarian, to name just a few. All of these and more are on display in Alison Klayman's 2012 film *Ai Weiwei: Never Sorry*, a film worth watching in its own right. *Human Flow*, however, is not a film *about* Ai Weiwei but rather a film *by* him, one that focuses on the global migrant crisis and one that visually and viscerally shows the sheer inhumanity of so much humanity in motion. There are many other movies that have focused on the link between injustice and humanity in motion—*Rabbit-Proof Fence* (2002), for example, chronicles the story of two aboriginal girls trekking across Australia to find the family they were taken from as part of Australia's aboriginal "relocation" (stolen

generation) policy, while *El Norte* (1983) tells the story of two
teenagers fleeing Guatemala on a perilous journey north-
ward to the United States. But Ai Weiwei as a visual artist
prefers to let images tell their own stories. While watching
this film, all sorts of questions will run through the viewer's
mind: Why are so many people leaving their homes? Why is
so much of the world complacent or indifferent in the face
of this injustice? What happened to the human spirit in the
heart of humanity? With refugee and migrant populations
growing rapidly around the world, and with many countries
closing their borders (and many people closing their hearts
and minds), Ai Weiwei's film is a defiant reminder that this
is not a story of us and them, but rather simply a story of us.

⊨⊣+ +⊢⊨

Tunes

Finally, here's some music to help get you into your legal
groove, should you need any assistance in doing so. It goes
without saying that you should not illegally download any
of these.

Once again, as a reminder, I will be recommending
songs that don't normally or predictably show up on playl-
ists about law and justice. "I Fought the Law" is a great song,
whether it's the version from the Bobby Fuller Four, The
Clash, or Green Day (I consider The Clash's version the
best), but it's such a painfully obvious choice that there's no
point in recommending it here. The same is true of a song
like Bob Marley's "I Shot the Sheriff," which is of course an
amazing song but again, a very obvious selection for a playlist about the law, so I'll leave that one off, too. Same with

other classics like Jay-Z's "99 Problems" or Snoop Dogg's "Murder Was the Case."

Then there are songs that may be of use during your study of law, but aren't really about the law at all so I won't recommend them here, either. Bruno Mars' "Uptown Funk" has nothing to do with law, but on your bad days in law school it will help you change the negative energy of the first F-word that came to mind into the positive energy of another, egregiously more danceable one. When you're trembling with trepidation as you approach the bench to argue your case in moot court as a 1L, if you imagine yourself saying "Your Honor, May It Please the Court, I'd like to Uptown Funk You Up," all your stress will melt away. Unless of course you actually *use* that as your opening line, in which case your moot court experience will undoubtedly end in stressful disaster, leaving you in a decidedly different sort of funk.

So without further ado and delay, let's get started with our list of non-obvious tunes about law and justice.

Ana Tijoux, "Antipatriarca" (2015)
There are so many other songs I could recommend from Chilean-rapper Ana Tijoux, but I'll start with this one and let you discover the rest of her catalog on your own. For this song, Ana Tijoux delivers a song of empowerment for women around the world, channeling South American musical vibes all along the way. Whether you're in the mood to study and explore women's rights or human rights, or even indigenous rights (Ana Tijoux in recent years has become involved in indigenous rights issues in Chile), this song is an amazing way to start your inspired study session.

Junior Murvin, "Police and Thieves" (1976)
Before you start soiling your pants and foaming at the
mouth in rage at me for recommending what you might
think is too obvious a song for this list, let me explain why I
have good reason to include this classic from Junior Murvin.
First off, please do note that I am recommending the original version, and not the 1977 remake by The Clash (which
is also good, but so different from the original as to be seen
really as a completely separate song). Secondly, how could
I not include at least one reggae song on this list? It's genuinely unfortunate that so many so-called aficionados of reggae don't understand both the spiritual and political forces
that came together to create reggae music. No, reggae music isn't about smoking weed and chilling out. Reggae was
forged from the deeply spiritual roots of Rastafari and then
combined with the poetic mettle of those unsung Jamaicans
who fought tirelessly to rise up their lives while living in a
political system that wanted only to drag them down. When
Junior Murvin sings "From Genesis to Revelation, the next
generation will be, hear me," we don't just hear him, we feel
him and we feel his defiant message of hope.

Superman Is Dead, "Sunset di Tanah Anarki" (Sunset in
the Land of Anarchy) (2013)
Indonesia is a wonderfully musical place. The current president of Indonesia, for example, Joko Widodo (aka, Jokowi),
is a big heavy metal fan who claims that his commitment to
democracy was inspired in part by the band Metallica. Not
kidding, either. Superman Is Dead, on the other hand, is
a band that came straight outta Bali and still remains the
most eloquent expression of Indonesian punk there is (yep,

Indonesian punk is a thing, as is Indonesian reggae—just check out Ras Muhamad from J-town, aka Jakarta). This song is in many ways about justice battling injustice, about human rights and law bringing order to a land where corruption and abuse of authority have brought so much disorder and anarchy. If you watch the video for this song, you can see images of Munir Thalib, an Indonesia human rights activist who was assassinated in 2004. If you're a fan of Green Day, you'll no doubt love Superman Is Dead. So put on this tune, order up some *nasi goreng*, open your human rights textbook, and start making the world a better place already.

Eric Wainaina, "Nchi Ya Kitu Kidogo" (2001)
Transparency International has been arguing for years that widespread corruption is more than just a nuisance or inconvenience. It's a full-fledged human rights violation that undermines the rule of law and ruins lives. Of course, if you live in a place where corruption is endemic, you don't need Transparency International to tell you what you already know. If you live in a place like Kenya, you need Eric Wainaina to turn resentment into rhythm, and the result is this wonderful tune about pervasive corruption. The title of the song translates (from Swahili) as "The Land of Petty Bribery," and it is difficult to describe how deeply this song resonated with so many Kenyans (and others) and how deeply this song was despised by so many Kenyan officials. Don't let the very danceable music fool you—this is a powerful anthem against corruption and the officials who, in engaging in that corruption, continuously break the very laws they are supposed to uphold and protect.

Te Vaka, "Sei ma le losa" (2002)
The first time you hear this song, you'll end up with goose-bumps, a few tears, and a persistent disbelief that music so beautiful could be made by humans. But made it was, and by the very human group Te Vaka, whose members come from various parts of the Pacific Islands. This song in particular, the title of which translates loosely as "Here with this rose," was written in memory of David McTaggart, one of the founding forces behind Greenpeace, who had died in a car accident the year before. For obvious reasons, protection of the environment is a huge issue in the Pacific Islands, and here is a song to remind everyone just how much would be lost if the Pacific Islands become ruined by the many environmental problems, including nuclear contamination, that threaten the region. This is the perfect song to help you develop an interest in environmental law and an appreciation for the Pacific Islands.

A-Rühm, "Popmuusik" (1998)
No playlist is truly complete without some old-school Estonian hip-hop, so allow me to present A-Rühm and their song "Popmuusik" in all its Estonian glory. If you aren't familiar with the music scene in Estonia, you should know two things about it: (1) it's amazingly rich and has been so for pretty much all of Estonian history, and (2) it gets caught up in calls for rights and justice with amazing ease. Hip-hop is a relative newcomer on the Estonian music scene, and given the long history of folk music in Estonia and the long menu of other Estonian music genres I could have drawn on, I fear greatly that my Estonian friends will pummel me with potatoes when they see what I have done here. What

can I say? *Andeks.* There's nothing in the song itself that's inherently focused on the law. It's mostly a rude rant about crappy Estonian pop music. What makes this song a song about rights and justice is simply what it is. First, you take a musical genre—that would be hip-hop—with deep roots in the expression of discontent and the demand for equality, dignity, and justice. Next, you re-route it to Estonia, where fluid lyrical traditions meet a political moment when Estonia is once again stretching its political wings toward freedom and democracy. Finally, you end up with a song that on the surface is an open complaint about the poor quality of Estonian pop, but in the larger sense, is a democratic celebration of the right to complain, the right to be different, and also a call for Estonia to do a better job with its politics than it does with its pop music.

Peter Gabriel, "Biko" (1980)

In the discussion of *Django Unchained* in my movie recommendations, I also mentioned a film called *Cry Freedom*, about the life of anti-apartheid activist Steve Biko. The inimitable Peter Gabriel wrote this song about Steve Biko, not just about what happened to him, but about how his defiant spirit and anti-apartheid struggle would both carry on long after he was gone and would ultimately win the heart of humanity. There's more to the song than just the content itself, which from a musical and lyrical point of view, is formidable in its power. The global anti-apartheid movement that slowly came together in the 1980s was one of the first to unite musicians across continents to harness the power of art and music in order to mobilize people in the fight for justice. Peter Gabriel's song was one of the first to herald this global movement, and it remains to this day one of the finest. Unlike other musicians who joined in the tide of the anti-apartheid movement merely to capitalize on its popularity or to use Africa's misfortunes for their own personal gain, Gabriel knew from the start that this was quite rightly an act of collaboration and not of charity, that there was as much to share with African musicians as there was to learn from them. When you're having a cynical moment in your legal studies, or aren't sure whether law school is for you, listen to this song and especially to the final refrain, "And the eyes of the world are watching now." Injustice is everywhere in the world—this is a song that reminds us to be ever vigilant, and a song that reminds us that law is forever the harbinger of justice.

EPILOG

FROM PERPLEXITY TO CLARITY

And with that, it's time to bring everything to a close. I started this book as a guide for those perplexed by law school, muddled by questions of what studying and practicing law were all about. I hope at this point you've found some clarity where before there might have been only perplexity. Remember, too, that this little tome was not intended as a recruitment tool for law school, but rather as a guide to help you make the best and most-informed decision about whether law school is right for you. Whether or not you decide to pursue the study of law, the main thing is that you feel you made the right choice. You'll never be completely certain, of course—no one ever is, especially about things like this. So if you're still feeling a little lost, you're definitely not alone, and if it helps, remember that if you say Lost School relatively quickly, it sounds almost exactly like Law School, and that can't merely be by accident.

Whatever it is you decide to do, make your choice fearlessly and in good conscience, and don't let doubts plague you. Law is one path to follow, but there are others out there, too, and one of them is exactly the path you were meant to be on. There's something to be said for finding that path, and, once you've walked a little ways down it, for never wasting time wondering if other paths might have been better. The real trick is simply to make the path you end up on the best path it can be. Far too many people walk blindly through life. Open your eyes and walk fiercely, whatever path you end up following. Do that, and I promise you that no matter what path you choose, justice will forever be your companion.

ABOUT THE AUTHOR

D. C. Zook is a writer, musician, and filmmaker who also happens to be a professor at the University of California, Berkeley, in the departments of Global Studies and Political Science. He writes both fiction and nonfiction, and cultivates both sense and nonsense. He is currently at work on two books, one on new frontiers of human rights and the other on the changing landscape of cybersecurity. He is also plotting his next novel, and plotting many other things as well.

Visit D. C. Zook at dczook.com

www.ingramcontent.com/pod-product-compliance
Lightning Source LLC
Chambersburg PA
CBHW061025220326
41597CB00019BB/3458